THE JOURNEY

*A Service Member's Memoir
from Vietnam to Iraq
and Everything In Between*

By Lt Col Steve Jacklin

> Honey,
> Enjoy the read my friend. There's a section on our Beirut cruise. Publisher made me take names out. You and Roscoe was left out.
> Semper Fi,
> [signature] — 2024

Some names and identifying details of people described in this book have been altered to protect their privacy.

THE JOURNEY: Copyright © 2021 Steve Jacklin
All rights reserved. Except as permitted under U.S. Copyright Act of 1976, no part of this book may be reproduced, stored in a retrievable system, or transmitted by any means without written permission from the author.

ISBN: 9798752583841

THIS BOOK IS DEDICATED TO
MY WIFE OF FIFTY YEARS
MY THREE LOVING AND SUCCESSFUL DAUGHTERS
AND MY GRANDCHILDREN NOW AND IN THE FUTURE

Contents

PROLOGUE i

Chapter 1   I'VE ARRIVED – *"WAKE UP FNG's, ONLY TWELVE MONTHS TO GO"* 1

Chapter 2 THE BUSH – *"IT DON'T MEAN NOTHIN'"* 23

Chapter 3   THE QUE SON MOUNTAIN - *"THEY CAN KILL ME, BUT THEY CAN'T EAT ME"* 37

Chapter 4   LEAVING NAM *"DEROS (DATE ELIGIBLE RETURN FROM OVERSEAS)"* 55

Chapter 5   I AM NOW A MARINE PILOT (Part 1) — *"HELICOPTERS DON'T FLY, THEY JUST BEAT THE AIR INTO SUBMISSION"* 71

Chapter 6 I AM NOW A MARINE PILOT (Part 2) - *"FLY IT TILL THE LAST PIECE STOP MOVING"* 85

Chapter 7 SPECIAL OPERATIONS - *"FINAGLE'S LAW OF DYNAMIC NEGATIVES."* 101

Chapter 8   THE OV-10 BRONCO - *"FIRST RULE, MAKE SURE LANDINGS EQUAL TAKEOFFS"* 113

Chapter 9 MY TEENAGE YEARS – *"IN A GADDA DA VIDA"* 125

Chapter 10 ENTER MY FOURTH DECADE - *"AS I COUNT THE RINGS ON THE TREE"* 141

Chapter 11 GLOBAL WAR ON TERRORISM - *"MAGNUM OPUS"* 155

Chapter 11A THE POLITICS OF GWOT – *"IF THIS WAS EASY, THE FRENCH WOULD BE DOING IT."* .165

Essay on THE DEEP STATE and the SWAMP CREATURES 175
Iraq's *Parade of Horribles* 189
EPILOGUE 193

Pvt Jacklin graduating Paris Island

PROLOGUE

The stories are my real-life events as they dig deep into my combat career as an enlisted Marine grunt, officer, and pilot. The book takes me from my bush days in Vietnam to my mission in Beirut and the invasion of Grenada. I write about the terrible day in September when four airliners attacked the homeland. I'm ordered back into uniform and performing duties in the Army Operation Center in the basement of the Pentagon later deployed to Iraq during the "Surge." I present the combat side of the GWOT and the political infusion of bullshit into war. The first four chapters on the Vietnam War were made into the hit musical "*WELCOME HOME.*"

      Born in South Carolina and the eldest son of a career military dad, I found myself changing residence frequently. I lived in numerous states, including New Mexico, Ohio, or North and South Carolina. I spent some of my teenage years in Tripoli, Libya, with frequent trips to Rome, Italy. You would think the early travels would slow my rabbit motor down and accept a more peaceful atmosphere. Not really. I spent the next fifty years in far-off places like Vietnam, Grenada, Kuwait, Iraq, Israel, Norway, Denmark, Japan, Okinawa, to name a few. I am unsure where this nomadic urge came from, but I wrote this book describing those travels with over fifty vignettes.

      I recall playing at an early age with my friends on the railroad tracks next to my house. We did the usual stupid kid stuff—played chicken with the oncoming locomotive or threw rocks at the Co-Co axle box. We would also exercise less brutish delinquency, waving at the train engineer to get him to blow his air horn. Almost always, we'd get a fist shake from the brakeman hanging out of his cab. We even had boyish discussions on hopping a flat car and riding to wherever the train was going. Fortunately, we never took that ride. We couldn't think it through enough to figure out how to get back home after our journey.

As my co-conspirators talked trash about growing up and becoming railroad cowboys, a compulsion would invariably pull me in another direction. After our railway games ended, I stared, sometimes for more than a few moments, down the parallel irons and wondered where the railroad tracks would take me. What would be the completion of the travels? I needed to find out what was at the end of the metal road.

My quest to find the end of the tracks, the top of the mountain, or what lies over the ocean horizon is where I sit today—an old fat white guy with a cornucopia of memories from those explorations. I've lived beyond any normal expectations, outlasted my shelf life, and had enough passion and love to last ten lifetimes. I am thankful for all I have, all I've done, and where the winds have taken me. I now find myself in a reflective period of what was, what is, and what awaits me at the end of the railroad tracks.

This writing was a journey that took me down those parallel tracks again. It triggered flashbacks of war's angry horror, life's ballbusting humor, and the passionate love that has lasted a lifetime. Putting one's life journey into twelve chapters and over fifty vignettes was heavy. Seeing faces gone was often a struggle. Reliving significant events of a nation's sixty-year history with the luxury of hindsight was complicated.

This literary voyage has been cathartic, pleasant, and palpable to my psyche. I would often find myself surfing the waves and hitting the pocket on a Kookapinto Longboard at San Clemente Beach. Then, I'd do a quick transition to the jungles of Vietnam or the desert of Iraq. The mind travels were fast and indisputable.

Thanks to all travelers, friends, and family that have made this crazy commute with me.

THE CLOCK

Time has changed and channeled the expectations
Now stop the clock roll back the afternoon
Relieve enhancements, manage relations
The lyre vibrates a sultry poesy tune
find rapture in the fullness of the moon
Can we wipe and clear the glad blissful trance
The beginning we will consummate soon
Three young voices a mercurial stance
Aged well not happenstance

Chapter 1
I'VE ARRIVED – *"WAKE UP FNG's, ONLY TWELVE MONTHS TO GO"*

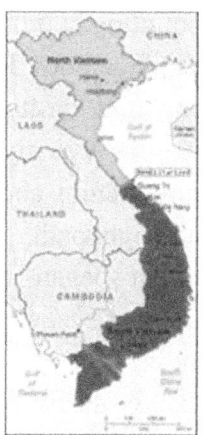

Arrive Vietnam

Reflection, June 1970 TWA flight 1369 begins its final approach. I was awakened by a "ding" as the cabin sign illuminated FASTEN SEAT BELTS. The NO SMOKING neon glowed. The Captain's voice was echoing through the cabin area, arousing the sleeping passengers. "We're beginning our final approach into Da Nang, South Vietnam's second-largest city. Stewardesses, prepare the cabin for landing, and thank you for flying TWA." Then he added, "Hope to see all in twelve months." Hope to see you all in twelve months, crap! Does he know something we don't know?

The Boeing 727 circled over the Gulf of Tonkin at thirty thousand feet for about twenty minutes. The Captain again got on the intercom and announced that we were "beginning our descent." The aircraft began a rapid drop toward what I hoped was the airport. As the jetliner accelerated in its downward trajectory, I noticed the expression on other passengers' faces. They seemed to be listening to their inner voice, "What if we crash and I die" and other premonitions like, "If I crash in the sea, will they be able to find my body and bury me in Arlington?"

The lance corporal in the aisle seat next to me began counting the number of rows in front of him to the airplane's emergency exit doors. My curiosity interrupted his tabulation. "What's the deal with the counting" I quipped.

He chuckled, "If the plane goes down in the water, and the lights are out, I want to know how far it is to the emergency exit." *This guy has got his shit together,* was my whispered thought.

We did a quick introduction and then sat quietly in our seats as we continued on our flight path toward what we hoped was a safe landing. This descent began my journey with Lance Corporal William Dalton, who became a friend, a battle buddy, and a conflicted consciousness.

Dalton was a thin, lanky Marine from Terra Haute, Indiana. Like me, he had been in the Marine Corps less than six months and was a grunt, a basic infantryman. We would soon share a fox hole and muse over our shared taste in music, sports teams, and blonde girls with long legs. Dalton said whenever he saw a good-looking blonde, he would immediately drop three rungs on the evolutionary ladder.

Later, when not engaged in killing bad guys (or preventing them from killing us), we passed the time bullshitting about the absurdity of our current predicament. But we were volunteers, not like Army combaters that were, one day, sitting on their tractors in Benton, Alabama, counting the corn rolls and listening to Buck Owens. Then the following month, drafted into the war zone, eating C-rations and hunting Viet Cong in the swamps of the Mekong Delta.

Dalton and I weren't sure there was a town named Benton in Alabama, but it didn't matter. We soon found out we had a lot in common, including our upcoming twelve months in the Vietnam bush.

Suddenly, a loud, alarming, screeching metal-to-metal sound filled the cabin. A frequent flyer next to me gave a nonchalant thumb up and smirked, "It's the airplane's flaps."

I wasn't sure what a flap was but obviously, from the frequent flyers' reaction, not the sound of a final death knell to my Hemingway Moment.

The next loud noise was the aircraft landing gear extending. It seemed longer than forever before a big thump would jolt me. Finally, we touched down. The plane appeared to decelerate with lots of braking, quickly veering its nose toward the airport terminal.

A salty veteran of the bush named Jenkins, beginning his second tour in Nam, smirked, "Wakeup FNG's, only twelve months to go." I began to unbuckle and move toward the exit while asking Jenkins, "What's an FNG?" Jenkins's reply was short and direct "Fucking New Guy." Yep, that was us.

I stepped out of the aircraft door and gave a sheepish grin to the last blonde-haired, round-eyed girl I would see for the next twelve months. As the stewardess gave me a perfunctory smile, I gave a sheepish, unconvincing thumbs up and continued down the stairway to the bottom, followed by Dalton and the rest of the newbies.

Once on the ramp, a loud sergeant made his presence known with the greeting "Welcome fresh meat" and then gave us contradictory instructions he expected us to follow. I just kept in the middle of the crowd and followed the herd; it seemed safer that way.

They said the summers were hot in Vietnam, or as bush veterans called it, Nam. But I wasn't quite ready for July's stifling, humid, scorching heat of the airport tarmac. The air was hot, sticky, and smelly. I was sure this was just a temporary heatwave, and things would get cooler once nighttime came. Yeah, right!

I had arrived, a Marine in a war zone, looking for my M-16, looking for bullets to put in my M-16, looking for someone to shoot with my M-16. Pretty gungy, but this is what I'd been training for the last six months. I'd just turned nineteen; it beat bagging groceries, doing real work on road construction, or taking college courses about real life. Hell, I was living in real life.

The loud sergeant started barking orders to us newbies. We were still dazed from a twenty-three-hour flight, and a "What the fuck did we get into" look was painted all over our faces. The sergeant directed the group to fall in, the military term for taking one's place in an orderly grouping of men and equipment. In this case, the formation was more of a gaggle than an orderly grouping of men and equipment.

Standing behind the sergeant were three non-commissioned officers from three military branches, Air Force, Army, and Marines. He turned the gaggle over to these three noncoms. The Air Force Sergeant stepped forward to collect the airmen in our group. He was "breaking starch" with his uniform, razor-sharp creases in the trousers and jacket, meticulously groomed with a cover (hat) sitting perfectly over his meticulously groomed hair. The group chortled with a few snickers as the Air Force Sergeant stepped forward. His movements were more sashay than a take command gesture.

Davis, another newbie, murmured under his breath, "Little Saint Sebastian." Most of us weren't educated or culturally sensitive enough to appreciate the humor. Later, I would find out the meaning of Davis' iconic witticism.

The snickers turned into jocular, whispered diatribes as the Air Force Sergeant began to speak in a Truman Capote voice. Having just read his book, *In Cold Blood*, I knew who Capote was and immediately linked Davis's earlier comment to a gender-bender ballbusting.

"OK, gents, please fall out and enter the bus on my right and take a seat; let's be quickly." Quickly, No shit. Saint Sebastian was getting his boys transportation on a blue air-conditioned school bus, and I would find out later the Air Force fought the whole war in air conditioning.

The Army was next to collect its quarry. A large black staff sergeant, probably a "shake 'n' bake" NCO, dressed in a short-sleeved khaki service uniform, a half size too small, and a large sweet spot under each armpit aggressively stepped forward. With a haranguing tone, he bellowed, "Army, get on the trucks, no grab-assing and take a seat." The Army's mode of transportation was a 2½-ton cargo truck. The soldiers broke rank, sprinted to the combat vehicle, jostled to get aboard, and found the wooden bench seat.

What was left for the thirteen Jarheads still in formation? Was it an air-conditioned bus, a truck to transport us to the war, or maybe base taxies? Hell no!

A Marine corporal, dressed in camouflaged utilities, Boonie hat, and jungle boots, stepped in front and gave us the news. "We lost our transportation Marines, so we have to hump to base operations for further transport. Pick up your gear, and we'll route step to our rally point."

Sounds easy, twenty-three-hour flight, no chow, tropical heat, humidity, and a middle-of-the-day stroll. Dalton murmured, "We didn't promise you a rose garden, just enough shit to plant one." OK, we were Marines, but that didn't stop us from bitching. With sea bags over our shoulders and field packs on our back, we began the one-mile hump to base operations.

Once we arrived at our destination, a cattle car pulled up. Yep, this was our ride, and we had ten minutes to relieve ourselves and get some water. Once ready, we boarded our ride to the 5th

Marine Regiment Staging Area. Arriving, we debarked from our transport and fell in on formation.

A crusty old gunnery sergeant came out and said a few words, nothing noteworthy, just told us to count one to three. Once we finished this cheesy "math for Marines" exercise, Gunny had the ones fall out behind him, the twos to his right, and the threes stayed in place. This counting exercise would determine our future for the next twelve months.

"Alright Marines, here's your assignment," The Gunny barked. "The ones to the first battalion, the twos to the second battalion, and the threes to the third battalion."

We trained as a unit for the last three months, and now they have broken up the team. We all wondered what kind of horse shit we were getting into.

We spent as little time as needed in Da Nang before helo lifting out to the bush. The Regiment wasn't going to waste fresh meat malingering on China Beach or shamming at the USO. Besides, quoting the WWI German aerial ace, Manfred Von Richthofen, when assigned mess hall duty, "I have not gone to war to collect cheese and eggs, but for another purpose."

We got transported to the airfield and boarded a CH-53 Helicopter, non-affectingly known as a "Shitter." The damn thing was constantly leaking hydraulic fluid in the cabin area. Note: If you rode in a Shitter and got off without any hydraulic fluid on your jungle attire, it was because the Shitter didn't have any hydraulic fluid left in its systems. No hydraulic fluid was not a good thing for continued safe flight operations.

The aircraft took off, climbed to six thousand feet, and proceeded to the regimental headquarters, in a hell hole, called An Hoa. With that forty-minute voyage, I could see green mountain vistas, wide flowing rivers, and valley lowlands pocked marked with craters architecturally designed by our bombs and artillery.

Without the rice paddies and greenery, the terrain looked like an Apollo 11 snapshot of the moon.

The Shitter did a quick turn to the left and awoke me from my daydream.

The crew chief said, "We're spiraling down to the landing area." I found out later a spiral was a helicopter maneuver that put the aircraft into a forty-five-degree bank, a one-thousand-foot per minute rate of descent with variable airspeed. The purpose of this maneuver was to prevent the bad guys from getting a bead on a slow landing helicopter.

Once landing at the LZ, the ramp to the back opened, Dalton and I unbuckled and departed, sprinkled with hydraulic fluid and bitching.

A very pogue-looking Marine sergeant met us. His apparel appeared to be new up-to-date fighting garb—flak jacket, hard hat, gas mask, M-16 slung over his right shoulder, spit-shined jungle boots, all gladly supplied by the military-industrial complex.

He led us to Headquarters, where we met our first sergeant, who gave us the usual screed with canned condemnations like, "You're now in Vietnam, don't be a hero, always walk where the man in front of you has walked and don't pick anything up."

After the Top's (1st Sergeant) haranguing, we moved to the supply hooch to receive our jungle gear. Then we went to the armory, had our rifles inspected, were given four boxes each of 5.56 caliber rounds for our M-16 rifle, then route stepped to a firing range and did a battlefield zeroing of our weapons. Now we were ready to go to war. Not yet.

Once weapons firing was over, we moved to the sickbay dispensary for our medical in-country orientation. HM2 Michael Richard Kempel, the platoon corpsman, was giving a lecture on preventing trench foot, the importance of taking malaria pills, and a class on the perils of syphilis titled "It's not all fun and games." Doc had a great sense of humor.

HM2 Kempel was from Cleveland, Ohio, and had been in Nam for eight months. He was a tall, thin sailor with thick glasses and a timid outward demeanor that belied his badass temerity under fire. Emotions harvested by months in the jungle watching Marines die, Doc would take the health and welfare of his Marines personally. With every death, we could see his pain as if he was the one that pulled the trigger or lit the fuse. Doc Kempel was one of the good guys.

The An Hoa airbase was encircled with fighting holes that Marines nightly occupied and performed sentry duty called "hole watch." Sentries stood vigilant over their sector of fire by peering out over the concertina (barbed wire). Any activity or movement seen inside the wire would have the Marine immediately sound the clarion call, "Gooks in the wire." We would arm the claymores, pop a lumination flare and take the M-16s off safe in anticipation of a kill shot.

Falling asleep on "hole watch" wasn't an option. To pass the time and stay awake, you would go to a happy place in your head and think about what (or what young lady) you would do when back in the "world."

All the newbies were assigned the duty of "hole watch." Welcome to Nam.

During these annoying assigned interludes, very little happened, except for a few incoming mortar rounds, occasional sniper fire, and "shitter burning" duty.

Shitter burning was a sacrosanct ritual of sanitizing latrines by removing the fifty-gallon barrels from the outhouses, pouring kerosene into the barrel of excrement, then lighting the fuel—the highlight of my Eagle, Globe, and Anchor career.

After two weeks of this undertaking, the first sergeant called me into his tent. "Lance Corporal, understand you have a military driver's license."

"Yes sir," was my reply.

The First Sergeant continued, "Need you to pick the Captain up at Liberty Bridge and return him to base. Any questions?"

Liberty Bridge

Fuck yeah, I had lots of questions. But proving I had my shit together and squared away was more important than getting all the details.

"No sir, ready to go," was my lofty response. Besides, I'd feel more comfortable asking a veteran in the platoon some of the minutiae like, "What's a Liberty Bridge, where's a Liberty Bridge and, who the fuck is our Captain?"

I check in with my squad leader, Sergeant Daniel Bennett, a twenty-one-year-old "Roll Tide" Alabama native. His eleven months in the bush hardened his persona and gave an outward appearance of confidence. His red hair and boyish looks were grizzled by the constant beatdown of jungle heat, sun, and rain.

He gave me the what, where, and who of the mission.

I hurried over to the motor pool to check out transportation. After signing for my M151 Jeep (that I didn't have a license for), I exited at An Hoa's west gate and started motoring along Liberty Bridge Road. *Hell, how hard could it be to find Liberty Bridge? The road is named after the Bridge.*

Looking at a topographical map, I figured it would take an hour's drive while keeping Charlie Ridge to my right. Beautiful Sunday drive with a full tank of gas, paid for by Uncle Sam. No one on the road, no one in the rice paddies. The weather was clear and dry. I wasn't stupid though, I had my M-16 at the ready.

Soon, I had the Bridge insight. I was accurate with my map reading, one-hour drive, and proud of accomplishing my first mission.

As I pulled up to the sentry guarding the gate to Liberty Bridge, he gave me an incredulous look and wanted to know what I was doing. I told him I was there to pick up Captain Branson and return

Repair at Liberty Bridge

him to An Hoa. The gate guard pulled back the movable barrier and continued to look at me like I was an audacious rube. I gave him a baffled look, then a head nod, and proceeded to the encampment at the edge of Liberty Bridge.

The Captain was easy to find from the description I received before departure from An Hoa, a large black man with captain bars. I quickly located the large black man with captain bars and reported to Captain Branson.

"Sir, I'm your driver sent from An Hoa to provide transportation back to base."

He acknowledged my salutation, looked around, and then gave me the same "what the fuck" look the gate guard did.

"Where's your convoy Lance Corporal" was his quizzical probe.

Suddenly, the light came on why I was receiving these doubting looks.

"Sir, I traveled alone."

The only thing the Captain said was, "Be in line with the convoy escorts leaving at fourteen hundred."

I grabbed some chow, talked to a few homies, and then moved my Jeep into position. In front of me were two duce and half trucks; in front of the trucks was a Buick (M-48 tank). An engineer mine sweeping vehicle was in front of the tank. Leading the convoy were four Marines walking point, carrying hand-held minesweepers and searching for land mines.

Epiphany! Like Icarus, my earlier hubris took me on a journey too close to the sun.

Later, I found out that the area where I did my solo joyride was very active with bad guys from the R-20 VC Battalion. In retrospect, a Sunday morning drive alone through hostile terrain with enemy ambushes, road mines, rocket attacks, and snipers was a dumb-ass stunt. Note to Lance Corporal Jacklin, lessons learned.

RIDE YOU SILLY TYRO

There's a point when courage ends
And stupid takes his turn
Battle on, with windmill songs
Nothing left to learn

There's a point when bravery turns
As foolish takes its place
Control the course with empty voice
A grimace on your face

Ride you Silly Tyro
If you make the Bridge
Luck has changed, as bastards fain
Gallop from the ridge

Ride you Silly Tyro
Only minutes left to go
Time will pass, then alas
Know what you did not know

There's a time when luck will stop
when committing such betise
move beyond and then respond
your ego's been appeased

Ride you Silly Tyro
Look back and see your blunder
The roads refreshed, with no regret
Time will put asunder

After a week of standing hole watch, we received a Frago (mission) to run patrols in Dodge City, a boo-coo fucked up place located approximately 20 miles south of Da Nang. Marines saw frequent booby traps, ambushes, and firefights there. We called this type of place "Indian Country," a free-fire zone with lots of action, just like the old west.

Patrol Vietnam

The VC (Viet Cong) and NVA (North Vietnamese Army) held strongholds and base areas in Dodge City. Numerous Marines had been blown away in this AO (Area of Operations). My

The Journey

anxiety, and at the same time, excitement level, shot up like a Saturn Rocket.

We drew chow, water, and ammo before moving to the helipad for transportation to my believed destiny. I loaded down with ten boxes of M-16 rounds, four grenades, a LAAW (Light Assault Attack Weapon), two boxes of C-Rations, and two canteens of water. The platoon sergeant gave me two bandoleers of M-60 rounds to hump for our machine gun team along with my gear. Heavy yeah, but what the hell? I was a Marine, young, and in great shape. Besides, the helicopters would drop us off, and we'd walk a bit, kill some gooks and get back on the aircraft; it sounded pretty simple, all in a day's work. Yeah right.

Our platoon commander, a new first lieutenant, was secretly nicknamed "Ricky Recon" because he was always jogging around the An Hoa airfield in a flak jacket and jungle boots. He showed up at the helo pad carrying a Thompson Sub Machine Gun, with ivory handles and ten magazines holding twenty rounds each. I knew I was a new guy, but this seemed "fugazi" (fake) even to me.

Patrol Vietnam

The Lieutenant gave us the details, at least what he knew about our mission. We broke up into lift teams and boarded the CH-46 helicopters (nicknamed Frogs), transporting us to the war.

The landing in Dodge City was uneventful, much to the dismay of the hard-charging nineteen-year-old killing machines. But I got the eerie feeling all would change, and it didn't take long.

We started our platoon patrols by moving in a staggered tactical column. The second squad walked point, with the first squad next and third bringing up the rear. Dalton and I were two of three new guys in the third squad.

We kept just enough distance between us to mass our firepower should we engage the enemy but far enough behind each other so one booby trap would not kill multiples Jarhead. We called it "spread loading the SGLI." Note: SGLI was the Serviceman Group Life Insurance program for military personnel that provided beneficiary death gratuity benefits.

Vietnam Patrol

Most of the terrain we patrolled in Dodge City was flat and dry, with overgrown elephant grass covering many parts of the AO. The elephant grass was razor-sharp and grew to over six feet. It would cut deep into your exposed hands and arms. The grass was a good cover from enemy snipers in the tree line but shitty when humping eighty pounds of gear on a hot, humid jungle day.

Sergeant Dan Bennett walked point, which I found odd since he was a short-timer having twenty days left in-country before the "Freedom Bird" would take him back to Alabama. He always talked about red Alabama dirt, his mom, and Merle Haggard. He also didn't want any FNG to get wasted on his watch.

As we meandered through the boonies, a loud explosion penetrated the jungle quiet. We were hit with the shock wave and immediately assumed a defensive posture.

Dalton and I both looked up into the open air and saw the lower half of a severed torso flying airborne twenty feet. We weren't sure who the unlucky bastard was, good guy or bad guy.

The next thing we heard, "Corpsman up." Another explosion filled the agitated scene; another partial body flew into the air. I started putting it all together and concluded that the good guys just got blown away.

Word came back to us that Sergeant Bennett and Doc Kempel got wasted.

It appeared Bennett, walking point, was blown away by an 82mm mortar round rigged as a command-detonated booby trap. We knew it was command-detonated because as soon as Doc Kempel sprinted forward to treat the wounded, the gook set off a second 82mm mortar booby trap, cutting Doc in two, WIA (wounded in action) five other Marines. In total, eight Marines from our platoon of twenty-three were either dead or Medevaced to the 95th Air Evac Hospital in Da Nang.

The executioner was good, very good. Charlie wired a mortar round to a firing mechanism then controlled it from a standoff distance. He set it up, anticipating Marines' foot traffic moving down the trail, and waited patiently for his victim, knowing the first blast would generate casualties and necessitate a corpsman to render assistance. The gook set the second one up to kill the corpsman once Doc got into the kill zone.

I thought targeting medical personnel was against the Geneva Convention; this sucked. Word got back to the third squad that even though Bennett was blown in two, he kept calling for his mother; this really sucked.

We got our payback a few weeks later. While running a squad patrol in the foothills of Charlie Ridge, we spotted four gooks moving through the ravine, one hundred fifty yards from our patrol. All four were wearing black pajamas, with two carrying AK-47's.

We immediately laid down a heavy barrage of fire, killing two and wounding a third, who got away with his buddy. We sent a fire team (four-man unit) into the ravine to check out the two carcasses and strip the bodies for intel.

We found out we had just killed a doctor and a nurse. They were probably being escorted to a field hospital by their weapons-carrying comrades. The doctor, from his name, was Chinese. The nurse was female Vietnamese, very young, very pretty, very dead.

As the naked, fly-covered bodies lay motionless in the ravine, a dark quietness pervaded the squad. The momentary enthusiasm we had at having just scored a kill began to be overshadowed by the realization one of the dead was a young female. The feeling didn't go completely dark as the squad leader reminded us of Doc Kempel getting blown away. "*It don't mean nothin'*." The patrol moved on.

A month later, Headquarters reassigned our platoon's AO, and we moved to a FSB (fire support base) called LZ Baldy. It had four 155 Howitzer guns and a couple of 81mm mortar tubes positioned on the FSB. Our job, of course, was to provide security. That meant hole watch and running patrols in the area to keep Charlie on the defense.

One such patrol started mid-morning with a platoon trip to the helo pad. We waited for about an hour. The weather was good, so the aircraft showed up on time. Two helicopters took us on a twenty-minute ride and dropped us off in a rice paddy at the bottom of a large hill with a good-sized acclivity.

Our mission was to hump up the mountain, look for Charlie and destroy any caches he might have.

After an all-day hump, we reached the top; no gooks, no-cache. The movement down the hill was quicker and a lot easier. Once we reached the bottom, I radioed to Headquarters, "Mission complete, negative contact," and requested our airlift back to base. That's when I saw God.

As we waited in the rice paddy, a VC sniper decided to have a cathartic moment. He let off a burst of automatic fire at our position. The rounds splashed in the water, five feet from my area, missing me and my quick trip to eternity. Seeing the bullets spray the water, I drove to take cover and somersaulted over a berm.

During my airborne ballet, the sniper let loose another burst of automatic fire, splattering right in the spot I had just launched from.

I felt something strike my helmet violently, jolting my head backward, knocking my helmet into the water. For a brief second, I was consumed by a sanctified peace, reliving my past life as it flashed in front of me while my ability to reason seemed to move in slow motion. The Valkyrie was making her decision.

I waited for a spiritual levitation toward a bright light. My prevailing thought during that nanosecond was, *So this is what dead is like?*

A head nod and a "Sorry about that" snapped me out of my eulogy.

It seemed my moment of death was only Sugar Bear kicking me in the head as we both jumped over the same berm. His size ten jungle boot to the side of my helmet was enlightenment.

From that point on, having just paid a visit to the netherworld, the afterlife and purgatory seemed less frightening to me.

We called in air support, and two AH-1 Cobra Attack Helicopters were on station within ten minutes. We marked the sniper position with a 40mm smoke grenade from a blooper. After clearing the Cobras hot, they began to light up the area with 2.75mm rockets and 5-inch Zuni's, looking like a grand finale on the 4th of July.

After expending all their ordnance, the Cobras departed for home, and we continued to remain on high alert.

Since it was getting dark and the pickup LZ was now considered hot, the helicopters and our transportation back to base would have to wait till the morning. No shit, now we have a slumber party in a rice paddy filled with bloodsucking aquatic leeches and other parasitic fauna.

We set up a defensive perimeter, maximized security, and waited until morning for our ride back to dry land. Hell, maybe Sugar Bear can kick me in the head again, and I can get a medevac.

After spending a few days in the rear to dry out, get warm chow, and clean uniforms, our platoon was assigned the area QRF, (Quick Reaction Force). Our job was to be on a thirty-minute standby and launch anywhere to assist a unit that needed reinforcements.

Acting as a blocking force while the attacking unit swept through the area was an excellent QRF mission. Holding a key terrain feature while the attacking unit moved into enemy contact was a great QRF mission. Pulling Recon Marines out of trouble when shit hit the fan was not a good mission, but we did that more often than not.

While standing QRF, we were assigned a mission and transported to a hamlet in The Arizona area. Rumor had it the "Agency" had just worked their Phoenix program in that area, focusing on this hamlet.

Phoenix was a CIA program designed to identify and destroy the Viet Cong via infiltration, torture, interrogation, and assassination. Torture, assassination! Hell, If the rumor is correct, we're about to pay a visit to some pissed-off villagers.

After we got off the helicopter, Dalton and I moved down a well-traveled footpath. We looked for ammo caches or signs of Charlie, food debris, feces, or matted down grass. Cautiously we proceeded; the hunt was on.

Suddenly, we came upon a fork in the foot trail. Dalton and I looked at each other for a half-second as if waiting for some divine intervention. There was no burning bush, no epiphany, no spiritual enlightenment to direct our next move.

I took ownership of the trail with a shrug and motioned that I would proceed down the right path, and Dalton nodded in agreement and pointed at the left fork. He gave me a thumbs-up, a pat on my shoulder, and went down his chosen pathway. With this, I would start my drift toward a decade of pseudo-nihilism.

Within minutes of our divergence, an explosion and "Corpsman up" rang out, followed by organized chaos. Moving toward the sound, I found Dalton being administered morphine by the corpsman. We began to set up a secure perimeter and call in a medevac helicopter.

Dalton was carried out on a stretcher after the helo arrived. He was anesthetized and lying motionless on his back with his left arm draped over his chest and his right arm curled up by his side. His body was charred, uniform torn, and bloodstained. His right boot and left leg below the knee were gone.

He laid silent on the stretcher while the medical team hurried him to the medevac helicopter. Loading him into the back of the helicopter was the last time I saw my friend Bill Dalton.

A Few days later, assuming Dalton was safely in a hospital getting primo care, I asked the First Sergeant, "How's Dalton?"

Without putting down his binoculars, the Top said, "He's gone." The inference was, gone from this life. That's how we did it in the bush, no memorial, no eulogy, no banal monologue of, "What a great guy he was."

The First Sergeant continued his binocular gook hunting. I walked away, emotions drained, having just heard Dalton got blown away. I began cleaning my rifle.

The ownership of the "path not traveled" weighed heavily on my conscience. I would be playing the what-if game for the next thirteen years. What if I took the left path instead of Dalton? What if Steve was ended? What if I did not marry my high school sweetheart and had three wonderful daughters? What would Karen's grandchildren look like or be like without Steve propagating the family lineage? Would she marry up into a better gene pool? This hereditary genome sequence was mind-blowing.

In 1983, after the Vietnam Memorial's dedication, I made a trip to Washington D.C. to visit The Wall. At the west end of the memorial entrance stood a podium with a book of 58,000 plus names killed in the war. I quickly perused the book, noting other Marine brothers lost, but could not find Lance Corporal William Dalton, USMC. This cutting realization was as if someone had thrown a large stone and hit the back of my head.

Dalton wasn't on the Wall; he wasn't dead. When I got the word, "He's gone," what the First Sergeant must have meant, "He's gone back to the states," not "He's gone, dead." Wow, a quick transformation in the thought process and a rewrite of history. What a head fuck!

Now it was Dalton surviving the explosion, losing a leg but living a fine Hoosier life for the last thirteen years.

I recalibrated the timeline and played the what-if game again. What if I took the left path, not getting blown away but losing my legs? What a "mad minute" this new reality presented in my psyche. It started screwing with my emotional tranquility, causing a gusher of surreal emotions, echoing a process of continuous reflections.

I wonder how my prosthetic life would have been the last thirteen years? I'm still married to my high school sweetheart, raising three wonderful daughters, and having a career selling insurance. But there would be no college football, no continued military career, no Pensacola pilot training, or a leather flight jacket with aviator sunglasses for me.

OK, so the left trail was not a mortal wound to Dalton but did have me rewriting my one-legged history.

After the 9/11 attack on our country, I was ordered back in uniform and on active duty. My assignment was to the Pentagon,

Washington, D.C. On a Sunday afternoon, I made another visit to the Vietnam War Memorial.

The Book of Dead was still on the podium near the Wall entrance, albeit with a few more names added since 1983. I bypassed the stand and went directly to The Wall with a different search query in mind. Staring at The Wall, I focused on the 1970 thru 1971 time period and read the names engraved on the black granite.

I saw the faces of Bennett, Kempel, Aston, Trotta, Tucker, Ward, Rowley etched on the stone embedded in my brain for the last thirteen years.

Then there it was. Like a physical reaction to having a tequila hangover at the same time, a linebacker slamming you to the ground. I struggled not to retch, my head was pounding, and a violent spasm overtook my body.

Daulton's name was engraved on the black granite, with the last name spelled with a U—D...A...U...L...T...O...N.

The what-if game returned with a vengeance. The explosion near a shitty little hamlet, in a shitty little country, did kill my friend, Lance Corporal William Daulton. The only thing that had changed from that explosive day, thirty-two years ago, was the spelling of "Daulton." The what-if game continued.

DAULTON

I knew a man from Indiana, Daulton was his name
A friendly smile, lanky frame, only claim to fame
We shared each other's memories
Thoughts would fill our songs
Minds were in the jungle, his heart's in Tara Haute

Steve Jacklin

Traveled out in search of youthful ideas
Filled our packs with comfort lies, water for our thirst
The times that were the hardest were the ones I remember first
Daulton smiled, took my path
Left me with a curse

Sometimes it rained so hard my tears
Would be disguised and hide the fears
Nothing would ever change the way I appeared
Daulton realized the lie, he was my brother dear

Trying hard to keep pace with changing scenery
Hacked our way through anger, frustrations greenery
I heard a sound, fell to my knees threw the helmet from my head
A quiet voice inside me said
"A friend of yours is dead"

Sometimes it rained so hard my soul
Would be soaked and bitter cold
Nothing would ever change the way it was told
Until that quiet voice told me, Daulton's going home

Chapter 2
THE BUSH – *"IT DON'T MEAN NOTHIN'"*

Dodge City Vietnam 1970

Reflection, August 1970, continued my first tour "in-country." Nothing's changed; the captain called us together and told us the obvious. "The more gooks we kill, the more gooks we have to kill, need body count." *It don't mean nothin'*. Charlie was formidable but not the water walking paladin Hanoi Jane, and her cohorts wanted to anoint. The body count would add up.

We were hot, humid, and always on high alert. But being a nineteen-year-old Marine in Vietnam was better than sitting in a liberal arts class hearing from a "never done anything" professor pontificating on Rousseau, John Locke, or Yoko Ono. I had just finished listening to "All Right Now" by Free on Armed Forces Radio. The splibs (black Marines) think there's not enough soul music on AFR. Being a Motown fan, I have to agree, but I'm not the program director.

The inner-city black Marines introduced a verbal expression into the Vietnam War, *"It don't mean nothin'."* This phrase made its way through the ranks to every one of us, becoming the footman of each experience too horrific to comprehend. "**It don't mean nothin**'" we would say, knowing full well it meant everything."

This double negative adage elicited passive utterance when witnessing or experiencing something so horrific that the psyche couldn't comprehend it. Grunts alternately used this phrase to express relief, even if they avoided being injured or maimed. Marines frequently used the phrase instead of "Fuck it," although the "F" bomb was also widely used in casual conversation.

I'd just spent three days in the rear. Yeah, right, the rear. A hill called an FSB (Fire Support Base) with tents and sandbags as home. Here's how that happened; someone at the TOC (Tactical Operation Center) took a topographic map and overlaid a clear plastic over the pending operation. Then they circled the tactical areas of maneuver. To support the maneuvering element, the Headquarters developed a fire support plan. Once completed, they found a hill with the highest elevated terrain in the AO (Area of Operation) in range of the maneuvering elements. They would blow the hell out of the hill to clear the trees and then insert a company of Marines for security. After security was in place, they transported in an engineer platoon to prep the summit for a larger LZ (Landing Zone). The grunts dug fighting holes and strung concertina (barb wire) around the perimeter, and Headquarters brought in a section of artillery to set up firing positions, wala! You have an FSB (Fire Support Base) or what bush Marines called "the rear".... no resemblance at all to any sanitized version of a John Ford 1940's movie. More like an R-rated Sam Peckinpah production.

Headquarters picked a hill that provided enough range for the 105 Howitzers to support the grunts when "shit hit the fan," and would need a little love from arty. The Howitzers provided a tasty carte du jour selection of weaponry, which included white phosphorus (known as Whiskey Papa or Wilson Picket), HE (high explosives), and illumination (known as basketball missions when dropped by aircraft). The faux lighting was excellent for night operations since night vision goggles hadn't been mass-produced yet. Had they been on the market, Charlie would be using them. The military-industrial complex would sell to anyone to plus up their quarterly earnings. *It don't mean nothin'.* I made a note to myself to buy DOD stock when back in the "world."

We received the command to saddle up; a phrase used to put your gear on and get ready to move back to the bush. We moved to our AO and set up for a couple of days, acting as a blocking force. What did that mean? Tactically, we'd take up a platoon position, dig in, set kill zones, establish fields of fire, and wait for the enemy to move into contact. In reality, it meant a lot of humping, wearing out your jungle boots, rainy days of boredom punctuated by forty-five seconds of chaos when Charlie walked into your kill zone.

You'd be humping into position, often up to four clicks (4000 meters) away from your FSB, with up to eighty pounds of gear on your back. Extra mortars, extra M-60 rounds, claymores, plenty of fragmentation grenades, water, body bag, and C-rations were the usual payload. You'd tote lots of C-rations since you may not get resupplied in the bush for days. That hunger hurt could be enough to make you want to kill someone; maybe that was the strategy.

C-Rations were canned food developed during WWII. Since they don't have a shelf life, the REMF's (Rear Echelon Motherfuckers) at Disneyland East (The Pentagon) decided to use the last war's leftovers to feed this war. The C-Rations cases were packaged with an assortment of meals, twelve meals to a case. You turned the carton upside down so as not to tell what kind of meal you were grabbing. The taste of the meal wasn't bad, with one exception. Everyone wanted to trade their "Beans and Mother fuckers"... a widely used colloquial term for lima beans and ham. Tough to choke down even when hungry. No one wanted fruit cake except for the machine gunner we nicknamed Beef, a bumpkin from a Northwest Virginia holler.

The Marines adopted a phrase called *ratfucking*. The term originated in the 1960s as political slang for "dirty tricks." The Marines added to the definition with the meaning "rooting through an assortment of items, only taking what you want." A case of C-rations would be frequently ratfucked, only taking the desirable meals leaving the rest for those that come late.

The Arizona Area of Operation

Once at the pickup LZ, the platoon was divided into lift teams. We had two choppers inserting the platoon into our AO (area of operation) called The Arizona, a real shit hole with plenty of trouble, bad guys, and surprises. The AO was located southwest of Da Nang and got its nickname due to its wild west nature and a free-fire zone. A week earlier, Bennett and Doc Kempel got blown away by a command-detonated booby trap in The Arizona. A few days back in this AO, Taylor took a 7.62 sniper round in the chest and got Medevaced to the 95th Air Evac Hospital in Da Nang. The round entered between the quarter-inch opening of his flak jacket, collapsing a lung and blowing out his backside just below his left rib cage. Good shot or unlucky bastard? We heard Taylor didn't make it. *It don't mean nothin'.*

Every Marine unit operating in The Arizona Territory had either been in a firefight or sustained casualties by booby traps. With fourteen members in a squad, you had roughly a six percent chance of becoming a casualty. Marines accepted those odds when they put on the uniform and chose to wear the Eagle, Globe, and Anchor. Pathological? Probably.

The helicopters inserted us into a rice paddy, fertilized with human excrement. Once over the LZ, the helo hovered three feet off the ground. We jumped off the ramp and sunk into the muck. The rice paddy was two clicks from our night position. Not only were we soaked from the waist down with shit water but we would have to hump nearly a mile and a half before dark.

Once clear of the rotors, we dispersed into a tactical circle, took our positions, weapons off safe, and waited to see if Charlie wanted to engage in any extracurricular activity. By now, after lying in a stale rice paddy for thirty minutes, we were ready for some action, hoping our squalid waterpark visit wouldn't be for naught. But, no contact. When all aircraft were clear and out of the area, we saddled up and moved to our night position.

On my first night in The Arizona, I was part of a three-man LP (listening post). The platoon moved into position for the night with a plan to search, in the morning, a river bed that had previously sighted bad guys. Since The Arizona was a "free-fire zone" anyone in the area was assumed to be an enemy combatant.

After we secured our platoon night defensive position, the Lieutenant decided the location of the LP. To be effective, it required us to set up with enough distance from the platoon perimeter to give warning should Charlie try and send a sapper (bomber) into our position with a satchel charge loaded with C-4. We would be on our own, tightrope aerialists operating without a net.

Not sure how I ended up on the LP that night. Maybe because it was my turn, or perhaps because my dumb ass volunteered. I found myself, along with two other Marines, getting gear ready to wander off approximately twenty meters toward perdition. The only question I had left was, "Who would Charon carry across the River Styx?"

The platoon sergeant made the final equipment check with particular attention to quieting anything that could make a noise. We left canteen cups and E-tools behind, with D-rings taken off our combat belts. No helmets, just soft covers on this junket.

Noise is our enemy, with hearing more acute at night. When the base sound level lowers with the external environment, our internal gain increases, making it easier to hear subtle, quieter sounds farther away. Damn, I never thought I'd be using that piece of eighth-grade science again. Glad I went to school that day.

Our movement to our night position was slow, muted, and deliberate. Once reaching our predetermined hotspot, we settled in with a radio check. "Breaking squelch" on our PRC 25 radio was adjusted and volume set to a minimum. But still, the return radio check response from the platoon "Lima Charlie" (loud and clear) boomed. It sounded like I was at a Led Zeppelin concert, sitting next to Jimmy Pages' Marshal amp as he kicked ass with his EDS-1275 double-neck guitar, exploding into the bridge of "Stairway to Heaven." Get the point? Clangorous!

Every part of my body was on high alert. The mission over-activated my neurons and stimulated my senses. The Arizona exhibited an unearthly vibe. We could not detect a sound except for B-52 bombers, known as "arc lights," carpet bombing miles away. No breeze rustling the trees, no nocturnal creature scavenging for food, no water rushing downstream. Should we hear a noise, our assumption would be "bad guys." The only other residents in our fighting hole were leeches and mosquitoes. The slimy bloodsucking leeches would crawl into our clothing and have a nightly feast. The aerial attacks from the anophelcs mosquitoes were relentless, halted only by the early sunrise.

Anticipating some action and a need to shoot straight, I slowed my breathing down so my M-16 sight alignment and trigger squeeze could find its target, one shot, one kill. My heartbeat pounded out of my chest, sweat dripped from my forehead, then rolled down my nose and into my mouth, giving me a sour, watery aftertaste akin to tasting like a dog sleeping in my mouth. The strange thing was, I was digging the whole trip.

The morning came without enemy contact. We radioed we were coming in and moved back to the platoon position. Even though we hadn't slept all night, we still saddled up with our squad to continue our journey. The platoon sergeant had a cup of C-ration coffee and shared it with our canteen cups. We also grabbed a few crackers from a C-ration box and slopped it with peanut butter. The breakfast cuisine wasn't tasty but did the job for a quick shot of energy. We humped another two clicks.

On Patrol

Walking down the trail in a staggered column, I was right behind the FNG (Fuckin New Guy), just out of charm school (an in-country orientation) and *gung-ho* to get his cherry popped. He volunteered to walk point. His name was Riley, a four-year college grad who we nicknamed GPA. During his four years in a high-priced, overrated institute of higher learning, he experienced student protests and classes canceled due to the SDS (Student for Democratic Society) riots and takeover of the college administration buildings, threatening the professors and staff. His formal education after his baccalaureate took a hiatus.

Riley thought all this pseudo-scholastic bedlam was ridiculous and, because of this anarchy, found the curriculum watered down, geared toward the loudest voices on campus. He knew this chaos stymied his formal learning experience, so after finishing his undergraduate degree, he opted for a master's degree in "life."

With his baccalaureate degree completed, GPA said he needed to complete his education and find out what all the antiwar commotion was. To fully mature, he felt he needed to experience a "Halls of Montezuma" moment. He didn't want a second lieutenant commission and a four-year obligation, so he took the enlisted route and a two-year sign-up. Back in the rear, we screwed with GPA. We told him to find a bucket and fill it with rotor wash, go get some "fallopian tubes" for the mortars, or see the supply sergeant and order five yards of flight line. He was good-natured about the ball-busting.

The cool thing about GPA, and other bush Marines that had a few years of college, was the pedagogic "rapping" they engaged in. Whenever we had downtime, a few of us would get together and "rap," taken from the word rapport. The conversation would start with someone bringing up a subject—meaning of life, marriage, colonialism, the hippy movement, who developed liquid soap, and why? Everyone engaged. It was like taking a course in liberal arts.

An example, when the subject of "getting blown away" came up, GPA expounded by quoting B. R. Ambedkar with, "Man is mortal. Everyone has to die someday." Shit! I just received three college credit hours in philosophy. Of course, we would paraphrase Ambedkar's, "We all die someday," with "*It don't mean nothin'*."

As we patrolled down the jungle path, my head was on a swivel, trying hard to maintain situational awareness and not let GPA do anything stupid. Then, as I stepped forward with my left heel, I felt an object under my jungle boot rotating slightly downward. Instantly my combat instincts mobilized, senses elevated with a realization I might be in a "shit sandwich."

My first thought, a Bouncing Betty! A booby trap, when tripped, the explosive charge was propelled 3 to 4 feet into the air, where the charge detonated, spraying lethal fragments above the waist.

Or was it a pressure-released explosive device where you armed the trigger by stepping on the plate? Stepping off the plate and removing the pressure from the device detonated the bomb.

In the bush, death is the constant default setting. But the thought of surviving the blast and losing your legs, or worse, having your genitals scattered amongst the elephant grass, was not a preferred way to show up at your five-year class reunion. Damn, so much for the high school football hero.

So, what's next? I halted the squad in place and motioned to Sugar Bear, the squad leader. He came up, and I advised him of the situation. After a "No screaming eagle shit" comment from Bear, he gave me that, now what do we do look. I suggested, "We treat this as a booby trap. Move the rest of the squad a safe distance yet still tactically deployed. Place flak jackets around my feet to decrease the frag pattern. Call in a medevac to be on standby and develop an exit plan."

Sarcastically Sugar Bear quipped, "Sounds easy."

With no further discussion, we placed flak jackets around my feet and lower legs. Once all the body armor was in place, I planned to dive out of the flak jacket encasement, stay prone on the ground, and hope for the best—the million-dollar wound, shrapnel in the buttock, and a trip to Hawaii for a three-week rehab. Worst case, I stumble out of the flak jacket encasement and absorb the entire brunt of the explosion. *What the hell? It don't mean nothin'.*

The medevac chopper was called and had an eight-minute estimated arrival. An LZ was identified and secured with green smoke on the ready. Once the bird was overhead, I would execute my best Sue Gossick, three-meter 1968 Olympic diving performance. Yeah, right. I'd be lucky enough to propel my ass far enough away to get a safe distance between the executioner and me.

As I stood there, careful not to release any pressure, a myriad of thoughts fired my synapses—Purgatory or Hell? The Stones or the Yardbirds? Katharine Ross or Natalie Wood? Have I kissed my last, have I sung my last, have I lasted beyond my shelf life?

The medevac helo checked in on-station, escorted by two snakes (Cobra Gunship). Expectations were if this was a pressure release device, the explosion would be instantaneous once I lifted my foot and released the pressure. A pool of blood, dog tags, and small chunks of body parts would be the only thing left for the corpsman to bag.

If a Bouncing Betty, once the pressure was relieved, the projectile would go airborne, take approximately two seconds for detonation; the guillotine would have done its job.

I did a quick head nod to Sugar Bear, letting him know I was about to jump out of the pile of flak jackets. I then gave a boisterous "Fire in the hole," and dove out of the flak jacket encasement headed toward Oahu or the afterlife.

I made a perfect landing, 9.8 score from the American judge with a 4.3 from the Russian.

While the "fog of war" consumed our staging area, an eerie quiet ate into the oppressive heat and humidity. Aside from the deafening raucous of my carotid artery, the only other sound was a "What the fuck" shout out from the tree line, then a breathless quiet replaced by nervous laughter.

With no explosion, body parts, or entrails scattered over the jungle path, we waited for a safe interval, then carefully moved to the displaced flak jackets. I intended to find the cause of today's disruption. We slowly moved the flak jackets away from the spot where I experienced my "Come to Jesus" moment.

One by one, we cleared the flak jacket area to inspect the impression left by my heel. I pulled out my KA-Bar, a seven-inch straight edge utility fighting knife, and slowly began to probe around the spot.

At first, I made large concentric circles, then smaller circles, each one getting closer to the center of the action. Within a three-inch radius, my probing hit her "G" spot.

My anxiety level shot up. I took a couple of deep breaths, and then I continued probing. I slowly placed my left hand over the incision, carefully brushed the dirt back, then moved my KA-Bar under the item and began feeling for electrical wiring. Nothing under the spot.

After minutes of not so assured self-assurance and frenzy probing, I reached the cause of our commotion, then used my KA-Bar knife to leverage the obscure device out of the ground. At first, gently, still unsure about its lethality. The KA-Bar's pace quickened as the item came into view.

There it was, the mysterious item that jacked up our excitement for the last thirty minutes, the conundrum that held thirteen seasoned combat Marines captive. The mysterious source of an old man's war story.... ***A damn C-ration can.*** The relief was as intoxicating as a contact high at a Who Concert.

With a few chuckles at the encounter, we saddled up and continued on our mission, keeping the world safe for democracy. Before throwing the can into the weeds, I took my towel and wiped off the mud to read the label.

There it was 'Beans and Motherfuckers' ... *It don't mean nothin'*.

Steve Jacklin

RATHER BE LUCKY THAN GOOD

Came to a crossroad, destiny's solution
The shaky smile told me which way to go
A racing heartbeat, drum-beating cadence
Destiny touched the water of my soul

If life would only give me two choices
Then I guess that I would
Disregard the expertise notion
Rather be lucky than good

Met a lot of widows whose husband has faded
Headstone epitaph all read the same
Here lies a good man expertise and jaded
Never known a lucky to die in vain

If life would only give me two choices
Then I guess that I would
Disregard the expertise notion
Rather be lucky than good

The Journey

Many the card been dealt on the table
Many the good man has lost his last dime
Many the talented person has faded
Many the experts have turned to the wine

If life would only give me two choices
Then I guess that I would
Disregard the expertise notion
Rather be lucky than good

Steve Jacklin

Chapter 3
THE QUE SON MOUNTAINS - *"THEY CAN KILL ME, BUT THEY CAN'T EAT ME"*

Reflection, October 1970, somewhere in the Que Son Mountains, somewhere around 900 meters, somewhere between "We're screwed" or "They're screwed." The mountains run northeast to southwest and border Highway 1 to the east. The "head-shed" (headquarters) was located at a major Marine airfield called An Hoa, to the west of the hills and an LZ (Landing Zone) called Baldy, to the east.

The foothills, called Charlie Ridge, was a ridgeline extending through the middle of the mountain range. Since it was only twenty miles south of Da Nang, Charlie could launch boo-coo (many) 122mm rockets into the Da Nang airfield if left unsecured.

Whoever controlled Charlie Ridge had good terrain elevation to keep an eye on The Arizona, a significant badlands with lots of trouble for Marines. Because of the strategic advantage of holding Charlie Ridge, the VC (Viet Cong) and NVA (North Vietnamese Army) continually engaged in firefights with Marines to control and hold certain positions on the ridge. Lots of Marines and lots of bad guys were blown away during those intermural games.

I found myself atop a hill in the Que Son Mountains. Operations had a tactical name for this shit hole, Hill 845, and some pogue (person other than a grunt) in Da Nang designated it LZ Rainbow, but we called it Vulture. Not for any gungy reason; we just felt like calling it Vulture.

Lovely place with steep elevated terrain, thick jungle brush, and monsoon rain beating down so hard you couldn't see ten meters in front of your fighting hole. Hell, you wouldn't notice Charlie if he crawled into your foxhole, made you coffee, and whispered Barry Manilow lyrics in your ear. As far as keeping dry, it never happened during the monsoon season, April through October. Always wet, always cold, always pissed off. So how did I get here?

LZ Vulture

I spent two days (and nights) sitting on the ramp at LZ Baldy, waiting for the helos to take us somewhere. Yeah, I know, hurry up and wait. We'd catch some z's by lying down and leaning back on our packs, putting our helmets over our faces to keep the rain from cutting into our cheeks, and mentally go to a happy place. The happy place usually consisted of the three B's—Beer, Babes, and Ball games. We'd send our cognitive state on an R&R, if only for a nanosecond.

Occasionally, the woolgathering would include trips home or what we called *The World*. But never would the momentary dreamy delusions include tactical maneuvering or fire support plans. We just needed a break from the war, and lying on a Marston Mat, waiting to be delivered to our next firefight, provided the opportunity for a brief escape.

Lance Corporal Robert Gordon (Gordo) Vincent settled in next to me and began a conversation about his family farm in Iowa, now run by his older brother and two sisters. Gordo was a good guy, liked by all. He was always alert and up to date on what was happening. He didn't have a steady girlfriend back home but said he dallied with a few young ladies from his graduating high school class prior to joining the Marines. Gordo seemed steady but, unbeknownst to us, would frequently battle demons.

We never knew where we were going until loaded aboard the aircraft. Two reasons for this—one, there were too many zipperheads inside the wire that might overhear someone running their mouth and tell their VC cousins what we're up to.

The second reason, not censoring our mail. Before 1969, a *REMF* (Rear Echelon Mother Fucker) would read and censor our mail and then blackout what he thought had compromised military secrets before delivering it to the bush. This censoring policy was changed by the Pentagon in early 1969, with the mail arriving uncensored. Because of this policy change, the Colonel thought it best to treat us like mushrooms, *keep us in the dark and feed us shit* until the last minute. Damn, we might tell someone in Berea, Kentucky, we were attacking hill 846.

We waited for our helo's, bitching about three things we could always count on from the Air Wing.

One, they never picked you up if it was raining. You'd sit there in the downpour, waiting for the clouds to lift or the visibility to clear.

Two, they always dropped you off either in a rice paddy or at the bottom of a hill. If you weren't wet before you leaped off the ramp, you were after you crawled out of the bog.

If not dropped off in a rice paddy, they would drop us off at the bottom of a hill. For some tactical reason, the concept was to walk up the mountain and catch Charlie at the top. Not sure it occurred to anyone that all Charlie had to do was walk down the backside of the hill.

And the third thing the Air Wing was known for, never resupplying us with food. They flew in plenty of ammo or C-4, but chow seemed to be the last thing to make the resupply run.

They airlifted us to an LZ on Vulture, occupied by another platoon, where we executed a tactical maneuver called "relief in place." The helos would land, drop us off, and the relieved platoon would get on the aircraft. The helos would take off with the outbound platoon while we laid quietly on the ready.

Thinking all the Marines had gone on the outbound helicopters, Charlie would come into our perimeter to scrounge for food; they were hungry too. We set up our ambush and waited for the bad guys to come into Sugar Bear's "kill zone"; the M60 machine gun team would have a *target-rich environment*. But this time, Charlie didn't take the bait. After an hour of quietly waiting for our prey, we sent a fire team (four men) down a trail to check things out.

Gordo was walking point, and within fifteen minutes, he had contact and was "busting caps." A quiet pause ensued, and the fireteam came back into the perimeter. They had one kill with two other NVA *di di mau* (bugging out) down the path away from the contact.

Before leaving the carcass, the fireteam did the usual body count routine—stripped the corpse, ratfucked his pack, searched his uniform for any intelligence value, and noted any unit patches on the uniform.

The NVA would attempt to retrieve the body once they were sure it was safe, could be that night, could be weeks. We'd know when they snatched the body. The stench of the dead NVA would permeate the whole mountainside. Dead people emitted a distinct rancid smell. Dead people left in the jungle for any length of time emitted an overwhelming rancid smell. We learned a few things from this encounter, Gordo was quick on the trigger, and the NVA had at least a battalion somewhere in our AO (Area of Operation).

Our *Kit Caron Scout* (South Vietnamese soldier) went through the KIA's gear. We learned who this unfortunate dead

The Journey

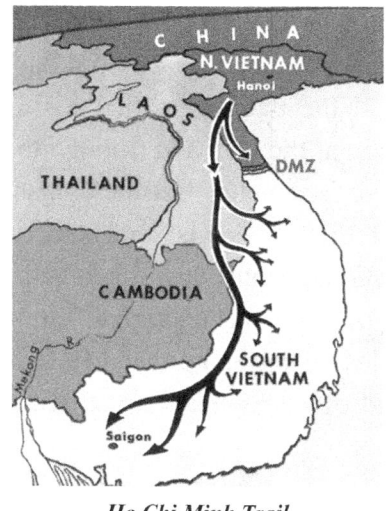
Ho Chi Minh Trail

bastard was. His ID and personal effects recovered painted a picture of a nineteen-year-old private first-class soldier. He had recently joined his NVA battalion, the V25 Infantry. He traveled for six weeks through Laos and Cambodia using the Ho Chi Minh Trail as the main artery. He then traversed the numerous mountain ranges to arrive, reporting for duty, anxious and ready to kill Marines.

He had a name we couldn't pronounce, but we didn't give a damn, we just called his Spiro, after VP Spiro Agnew. He carried a picture of what could have been his sister or girlfriend. Was this a picture of his wife? Did he have any children, an unspoken inquiry?

He wore a black watch on his left hand and a pewter ring on his right index finger. He had a partially written letter to someone of significance. From the tone of his letter, he wasn't sure if she was romantic or platonic. But since his rendezvous with Lance Corporal Gordon Vincent on a mountain trail in the Que Son Mountains, he would never find the answer.

He had two bullet entrance wounds in his chest and one exit hole in the back, just below the left scapular. He was dead, very dead, without having the opportunity to kill Marines. *Xin loin* (Sorry about that), *it don't mean nothin'*.

Our Lieutenant was "squared away." He carried a CAR-15, could read a map, call in artillery, and seemed to make the right decision most of the time, avoiding the stupid stuff newbies made. Not too gung-ho but aggressive enough to take the fight to Charlie. His pugnacious attitude was expressed with the combat mantra, *"they can kill me, but they can't eat me."* It pretty much said it all.

On our second night on the hill, he decided we needed a three-man LP (Listening Post) set up down the path away from our position. Since it was my turn to lead the patrol, I called for a huddled to start the planning. We looked at the map and decided to set up the LP twenty meters from our perimeter, outside Sugar Bear's M60 machine gun position. I picked Travis, nicknamed Alamo for apparent reasons, and McGinnis, nicknamed Mac, to join me in this soiree. Alamo was OK with the nocturnal jaunt down the hill. McGinnis had an attitude and seemed pissed off, but then again, Mac always seemed pissed off. He needed an attitude adjustment.

Before sunset, we checked our gear, ensured correct radio frequencies, and proper password/challenge for the day. We moved to our departure point at nautical twilight, briefed Sugar Bear we would be camped out overnight just in front of his position. If we made contact, we'd be hauling ass back into the platoon area. I told him to have his gunners secure their claymores, put the M60 on safe, and don't lite us up as we sprinted back into the perimeter.

We again confirmed the password/challenge, this time with the M60 team gunners, and quietly moved toward our night gala. Once arriving at the LP sight, we went to work. Alamo set up a claymore down the trail and took the clacker off safe. We crawled into the prone firing position, turned on our inner gook radar, and dialed up our tympanic cavity cochlea for max auditory reception. Showtime!

Quiet! Damn, it was quiet. Mosquitoes dined on any exposed flesh. We didn't wear mosquito repellent on night operations. The *bug juice* would mix with your body's sweat and provide a unique odor. With the right wind condition, Charlie could smell the ambush. So, we just laid there motionless, quietly providing an *all-you-can-eat banquet* for the blood-sucking party crashers.

The Journey

About forty minutes into the all-nighter, we heard a noise at our twelve o'clock position. It could have been a rat, could have been a rock ape (for those that believed in them), could have been a sapper with a ten-pound charge of C-4 on his way to take out Sugar Bear's machine gun team.

We go from DEFCON 3 (Defense Readiness Condition level 3) to DEFCON 1 in a micro-second. Weapons were off safe with fingers gently embracing the triggers, as smooth as making a winning putt on the eighteen green of the Masters' Tournament.

Suddenly, McGinnis lets out a burst of automatic fire, followed by Alamo lighting up the kill zone. I still hadn't made any visual contact, but it didn't matter; we had a firefight. I emptied a magazine and reloaded it.

Bush Marine

We began our rehearsed egress back to the encampment, Alamo first, with cover from McGinnis and me. Once Alamo was clear, Mac broke contact and hurried back to the platoon perimeter. After both were a few seconds removed, I blew the claymore, tossed a grenade, and ran back to our position, faster than Bullet Bob Hayes' 1964 100-meter Olympic gold medal win.

Safely back in the perimeter, the Lieutenant wanted to know what had happened. All I could report was McGinnis heard a noise, set off the ambush, and we all hauled ass back to the platoon. I heard the noise but did not get a visual confirmation.

The platoon remained on high alert all night. In the morning, we sent a fireteam down the hill to the LP position. They came back with negative contact and no visual signs of enemy action.

Since McGinnis set off the ambush, we concluded he was pissed off at being on the LP and wanted to come in. But then again, he always seemed pissed off. Honestly, we didn't understand his attitude; wet, cold, lying on the ground at night, pitch black, mosquitoes feasting on the back of your neck, and someone trying to kill you. Really, what's there not to like? McGinnis needed an attitude adjustment.

A few years later, I would learn McGinnis had become a game show host on a regional TV station. That sounds about right.

Few days passed without anything of note. Day patrols up and down the mountainside, night ambushes without contact, rock apes (for those of us that believed in them) throwing rocks. Rats, small dogs size, would crawl into your fighting hole to keep dry and look for food.

On one occasion, a little macabre humor hit the platoon. This humorous event, *The Episode of the Blooper Round,* caused continuous laughter and ballbusting for the rest of our stay on Vulture.

The M79 Grenade Launcher got its name, Blooper, from the sound the round made exiting the barrel ... bloop. The Blooper is a single-shot, shoulder-fired, break-action grenade launcher that fires a 40mm grenade. Each fourteen-man squad had one Marine (grenadier) humping the Blooper. Jersey was our Blooper humper. He carried

M79 Grenade Launcher

an assortment of 40mm rounds, including smoke, illumination, gas, and high explosive.

The 40mm grenade round had a spin-activated safety feature that would not arm the explosive round until it left the barrel, rotated approximately twenty times, and traveled 15 to 20 meters downrange. This safety feature prevented the grenade from detonating as it left the barrel, killing the grenadier. This rotational safety feature with the grenade played an essential role in Jersey's life expectancy, his continued good Karma, the focal point of this vignette, and stories to come. It also provided a large cudgel used on Jersey for the next month.

It was early evening, the time when your eyes began transitioning from bright daylight to complete jungle black. Some guys would take their red lens flashlight, pull a poncho over their head, and try to improve their night vision, thinking they were enhancing their "rods and cones." There was some science in that, pioneered by the Air Wing flight surgeons. I just stared into the dark for a few minutes, and my night vision was fine.

Because of the gook we killed earlier with our "relief in place" tactics and the LP action a few nights before, the anxiety level was high. Everyone's anal sphincter was so tight you couldn't get a spaghetti noodle through it. Tension increased to maximum RPM after the battalion sent an encrypted communication on the PRC 77 (radio). Charlie was on the move in the AO. The Lieutenant decided to do a fifty percent watch, four to a position, two would crash, and two would be on watch.

Just before dawn, with the light beginning to move across the valley, we heard a sound down the mountainside in front of our platoon position. I was in the foxhole next to Jersey and saw some shadowy activity inside his position.

I awakened the rest of my team and waited to see what was going on with this block party next door. Was there a changing of the guard, did someone need to empty their bladder, or was it an enemy movement?

Everyone was quiet, breath-holding quiet, funeral quiet, time to say a Hail Mary quiet. Then we heard it, the cracking of a branch. The next sound was a "bloop." Jersey had launched a high explosive round from his M79 Blooper. Three seconds later, we heard a thud then a loud expletive.

The shadowy activity in Jersey's position now seemed to be on a chaotic pace, with more invective diatribes rolling out of the foxhole and a half-mumbled shriek, "GRENADE!"

My experience told me that once someone bellowed the mayday call "grenade," it would be followed by an explosion, killing or maiming anyone that couldn't get at least ten yards away.

Seconds passed, no explosion, no AK-47 fire, no "gooks in the wire" alarum, only eerie quiet.

The Lieutenant came up behind us and wanted to know, "What the hell is going on?"

I said, "I'm not sure, but it looked like Jersey had contact."

We both started crawling to Jersey's position when a crescendo of laughter pierced the morning hullabaloo. "No screaming eagle shit, Lieutenant," said Anderson, one of Jersey's hole mates. "Jersey fired off a blooper round. It hit a tree and bounced back into our hole. The shit-for-brains tried to kill me."

The M79 40mm round hit a tree in front of Jersey's foxhole. It didn't make the required twenty revolutions, so the safety feature was still active, leaving the grenade safe. The killer round ricocheted back to Jersey's foxhole, with what was now a dud, landing next to Anderson where the agog "fuck" was heard.

If life would only give me two choices
Then I guess that I would
Disregard all the expertise notions
Rather be lucky than good

Once we discovered the source of the morning's entertainment and Jersey's newfound religion, what to do with the dud was still an issue. The Lieutenant came up with the perfect answer (I told you he was squared away).

He called for a block of C-4, a detonation cap, and a det cord. We cleared the area, place the C-4 with the selected widgets next to the dud, and lit the det cord.

"Fire in the hole" rang around the perimeter. An explosion was followed by a shock wave and an impressive plume of smoke and dirt filling the area.

That was it, time to light up some C-ration coffee and turn on Armed Forces Radio. They just happened to be playing *"Light My Fire"* by the Doors, no shit. *It don't mean nothin'*, just another day at the office.

Platoon

Charlie owned the night, and for Marines, nights in the bush had an elevated vulnerability in its blackness. With the action, uncertainty, and fear of the unknown, the stress would be oppressive, and for some, a challenge. But one evening seemed darker than most.

Lance Corporal Robert Gordon (Gordo) Vincent was a squared away Marine, reliable, dependable, and combat tested. His attitude was always confident and constructive, an asset to the platoon. That's why an evening's installment of *Battlefield Acrimony* surprised us and brought everyone to their knees.

Each Marine felt the pressure in different ways and would find their own coping mechanism. Gordo decided to handle the situation using his own baneful coping device.

Earlier in the week, a resupply helicopter came in with the red mailbags. The platoon sergeant opened the bags and five minutes later, "mail call" was over. Gordo received a letter, the first letter anyone can remember Lance Corporal Robert Gordon Vincent receiving.

No one noticed his change of attitude and vacant expression after the mail call. Gordo's normal casual conversational tone began to change, focusing on the pending Marine withdrawal from Vietnam. He ended every soliloquy with a whispered, "I don't want to be the last Marine to die."

On a rainy, cold evening in the Que Son Mountains, Gordon Vincent's demons took control of his decision-making process. He crawled into his fighting hole, pulled a plastic bag filled with white powder from his rucksack. Shaking, he opened the package. He couldn't tame his spasmodic upheavals. He needed closure from the darkness he ascended into.

After a few deep breaths, he galvanized all that was left of his outer life to complete the intended task swelling up from his inner life. He had devolved into an abnormal mentation process that challenged his cognitive ability for rational persuasion. His life's spiritual formation was rendered mute. His puerile catechism offered no compromise.

He took the powder from the bag, inadvertently spilling some of the *skag* on the ground. Ignoring the spillage, he quietly smirked, "It don't mean nothin'." He inserted the powder into his nose. A heavy snort began his intoxicating journey to the final pacification of the beast.

After ingesting three more lines, the powder was gone. Gordo then pulled four red pills from his pocket, grabbed his canteen, and swallowed the quadruplet.

He scribbled a note to his parents and explained how and why he was committing this remediation. He asked them not to be angry and was sorry for the pain he knew his actions would cause.

He then leaned back on a sandbag, pulled his poncho over his head, closed his eyes, and quietly resigned.

Gordon was found in his rain-soaked fighting hole the next morning, face down, life having passed from his fragile, broken body.

A routine medevac was radioed in to retrieve the body. The helo would be arriving in three hours. A toe tag with Gordon's name, rank, and serial number was placed on his big toe. He was then packaged into a body bag and placed next to the landing zone. Once the medevac landed, Lance Corporal Robert Gordon Vincent, USMC, unceremoniously began his journey home.

> *Gordon made a house out of sandbags on the hill*
> *Then he made a home out of powder and some pills*
> *No one ever realized the pain he felt inside*
> *Gordon didn't want to be the last Marine to die*
> *He took a toke, wrote a note*
> *And quietly resigned*

Vulture was quiet for the next week, with a few patrols and LP's. The serene ambiance ended when a Shitter (CH-53 helicopter) dropped off an 81mm mortar team into our position for us to babysit. Just another pain in the ass we had to deal with, provide their security, and resupply both their food and ammo.

We now had an ammo dump full of high explosives, 81mm mortar rounds in the middle of our platoon perimeter. All we needed was a sapper getting into the wire and tossing a satchel charge into the ammo dump. This was as fucked up as *Hogan's Goat*.

The purpose of the mortar tubes being moved to Vulture was to support a regimental operation in the valley. We got this highly classified, tactical information from rumor control, usually more accurate than hearing from the head shed.

Sheltering these vagrants had the potential of becoming a real cluster fuck. Since we provided no direct threat to the NVA, they left us alone. But now, we sat on a hill with an artillery spotter, selecting targets in the valley, then raining down 81mm mortars on the bad guys or anything else the spotter suspiciously observed. The price of poker has just gone up for our platoon.

When calling into the rear to check on any resupply choppers, the battalion logistics officer said the helo assets were unavailable due to working the valley's tactical operation. Wala, he just confirmed the rumor control.

We were going on our ninth day without food resupply. We were good on ammo, frags, and of course, piles of mortar rounds. But we were missing chow and water. Guys got a little bitchy, more than usual, without no food.

We worked with the water shortage by taping creek water and purifying it with Halazone tablets but couldn't do much about the ongoing hunger nuisance. We still ran our patrols and burned up more calories. With no calorie intake, this only amplified the craving while accelerating the bitching and complaining.

So, what happened?

We had two patrols out looking for bad guys and ensuring Charlie didn't sneak up on our position. Suddenly a faint sound of humming rotor blades pierced the quiescent valley. Within minutes they were in view, two Shitters.

We immediately secured our position of loose gear. Landing helicopters would generate rotor wash that could blow up a small tornadic dust bowl causing damage to men and equipment. The battalion air officer was contacted on the aviation secure frequency and asked about the incoming birds.

The Journey

    Immediately we were advised the inbound aircraft were not for our position but were landing in the valley below Vulture. One of the active patrols radioed in and asked if the helos were landing at our position. They received a "Negative."

    As the Shitters circled to land in the valley, the patrols assumed they were chow resupplies and queried if they needed to hump down the mountain to retrieve any provisions. Again, the answer to the patrol was "Negative."

    The first Shitter landed in a makeshift LZ in the valley, blowing up dirt, creating a brownout. The second helicopter landed shortly behind, engulfed by the brownout. The Shitter's ramps came down, and ten Marines on each bird exited the helicopters' rear. Ramps came up, and the helos left the area. Unbelievable as to what we saw next.

    The newly arrived high speed, low drag, deadly Marine Warriors started to draw their equipment out of their traveling bags. One by one, the Marines pulled sheet music from their rucksack as musical instruments were retrieved from sea bags and placed in a formation.

    Falling in on the instrument formation, the Marines calmly picked up their melodious arsenal and began calibrating their weapons. Once tuned, they began playing a short program of John Phillip Sousa marches. Since this was the 1st Marine Division Marching Band, the ensemble concluded the recital with the Marine Corps Hymn. No shit, I was waiting for the high school drill team and cheerleaders to come running onto the field.

    Our ongoing patrols radioed in, incredulous of the music echoing through the valley and indignant that aircraft were available for this jungle concerto but not for delivering chow. I advised the patrol that they were on an open frequency mic and to take it easy on the four-letter words.

    Once the band finished playing, the Shitters returned, landed, their ramps came down, and the musicians boarded. The helicopters flew away, bringing the virtuosos back to a dry rack and a hot meal in Da Nang.

The platoon backlash from this boondoggle started with a series of "What the fuck just happened?"

It got back to us that Division was running a PSYOP (Psychology Operation) mission by playing marching music that echoed through the valley during the tactical operation. But being cynical and jaded by months in the bush, we all assumed the band members flew in from Okinawa to get a CAR (Combat Action Ribbon) and combat pay. One ten-minute gig in the Qua Son Mountains checked off both items on their bucket list. Without a doubt, a major FUBAR (Fucked Up Beyond All Recognition).

The next morning, we retrograded off Vulture and back to the rear, still hungry.

VIETNAM BLUES

I've got those Vietnam Blues
My draft deferment I will lose
Then I'll slip from the middle class
Get a bullet in my ass
I've got those Vietnam Blues

The war seemed justified to me
As long as it's on TV
Gotta go the draft is here
The wars unjust it now appears
I've got those Vietnam Blues

The Journey

My daddy said to me son
You don't look good with a gun
Let the poor boy be a fool
I'll even pay for your law school
He's got those Vietnam Blues

My mamma cried all night long
Said that I did not belong
Let another mother's son
Be shipped off to Vietnam
She's got those Vietnam Blues

Steve Jacklin

Chapter 4
LEAVING NAM *"DEROS (DATE ELIGIBLE RETURN FROM OVERSEAS)"*

Reflection, March 1971, I spent another shitty day in the mountains of South Vietnam. Everyone was pissed off more than usual. I couldn't tell if it was the rain, cold, or our continuous thirty-first day in the bush that affected the mood, *it don't mean nothin'*.

The Agent Orange aircraft made another aerial herbicide spraying over our position. We would get an inbound call with a ten-minute warning of aircraft overhead. We'd covered ourselves with ponchos as the plane flew fifteen hundred feet above us and started unloading its payload of dioxin. Once the spray had dissipated from our position, we took off our ponchos, wiped off the Rainbow Herbicide, and went about our daily combat routine.

Occasionally the head shed (headquarters) would order Marines to defoliate by hand areas around their base perimeter. Poor bastards doing the Agent Orange spraying always came back coughing like they had tuberculous or just smoked a pack of Camels cigarettes. This stuff was *bad juju*. If it did this good a job on heavy foliage, the question always was, "What did it do to Marines that breathed, ate, or slept in it?"

The Marines were starting to leave Vietnam. This pullout was Nixon's "Peace with honor" plan or what we use to call, "The gooks didn't win, the hippies did" policy. We won every major battle when we engaged the enemy. The problem was how we defined a win. The victory was as confusing as keeping score in a tennis match.

The reality was, it didn't matter to us. We were Marines, and Marines just did Marine stuff and left the scorekeeping to the *boo-coo dinky dau* (very much crazy in the head) politicians. Eighteen and nineteen-year-old combatants had enough to think about, how to set up the next ambush, where the day patrols would take us, and not dying for our country. We trained to let the bad guy die for his country. We were also thinking about serious stuff like how to kick "Jody's" ass (the man who romanced your gal at home) when we returned to the world. There was no time to think about politics, just our DEROS (Date Eligible Return From Overseas).

We finally pulled out of the bush and back to our fire support base, LZ Baldy. Upon arriving, we got the word our regiment was redeploying stateside. The 5th Marine Regiment had twenty days to pack their trash and move to Da Nang for transportation home. The first sergeant came to the platoon area with a caveat. The 1st Marines needed bodies. Anyone wanting to stay in-country could volunteer for a transfer. My first thought was, *What dumbass would volunteer?*

But as minutes passed, a compulsion came over me. I became one of those dumbasses that volunteered. I wasn't sure if it was a feeling of not wanting to be pulled in the fourth quarter of a big game or a deep affectionate Oedipus complex I developed for this

Hill 55

"Third World" bitch of a country. In any event, three days later, I was transferred to 1st Marines, located on Hill 55, to start my second tour.

Hill 55 was approximately 15 miles southwest of Da Nang, located 2 miles northeast of the Yen, Ai Nghia, and La Tho Rivers'

The Journey

confluence. The hill was a significant tactical firebase and had a storied history with the French, going back to the Indo-China war, 1948 thru 1954. While the French were trying to hold this stronghold, the Viet Minh overran the garrison and wiped out two "Frog" battalions. The French would get their asses kicked a lot whenever engaging in any gladiatorial scrimmages in Southeast Asia.

The Marines occupied Hill 55 and controlled it throughout their war in Vietnam.

Carlos Hathcock

One noteworthy chronicle of Hill 55 was the story of the legendary Marine Corps sniper Carlos Hathcock and his war with a female VC (Viet Cong) sniper known as *The Apache*. Her anonym was a nod toward the Apache Indians, known for their creative torture methods before killing their captives. One of *The Apache's* trademark techniques was cutting off eyelids and keeping them for souvenirs. *The Apache's* signature moves involved placing herself and the tortured prisoner within earshot of Hill 55 to make sure Marines heard her victim's scream.

On one occasion, she plied her trade on a captured private. *The Apache* tortured the Marine all afternoon, all night, and part of the next day. The victim's screams were heard on Hill 55. Marine units went to rescue the private but couldn't locate the torture site or were ambushed by snipers and forced to return to base.

The Apache skinned the private, tore out his fingernails, and emasculated the Marine prisoner by removing his genitals. Then she released her blood-soaked victim near Hill 55, screaming, running, and holding his organs. His journey to the base of the hill was visible to all the Marines at the firebase perimeter. He collapsed and died on the outer circle of the concertina wire.

The Apache's sociopathic exploits were a nightmare for Marines on Hill 55. Carlos Hathcock took her actions personally and spent weeks tracking her down. Finally, he spotted her with a four-man killer team, all dressed in black pajamas with bamboo leaf hats. At first, Carlos and his spotter, Captain Edward Land, had difficulty identifying the female butcher amongst the four hitmen. Unfortunately for *The Apache*, nature called, and she had to relieve her bladder. Once she squatted, Carlos had his prey. He took the bitch out with one round, from 700 yards, dead center in the chest. Hathcock's shot completely shattered *The Apache's* spine and blew out her lower backside. For insurance, he nailed her again with a second-round.

The Marine Sniper School in Quantico is named for Gunnery Sergeant Carlos Hathcock. A Famous Hathcock quote, "From a place you will not see, comes a sound you will not hear." The book, *Marine Sniper,* chronicles Carlos Hathcock's Vietnam experiences.

Even with Hathcock's perfect kill shot and elimination of *The Apache*, the stories of her butchery in 1966 stayed on every Marine's mind. It shaped our psyches and operating procedures in and around Hill 55. I always carried a fragmentation grenade in the left breast pocket of my flak jacket and was sure, instead of being captured, I would pull the pin.

The combat action on and around Hill 55 was uneventful, as discipline and unit morale steadily degraded. The stateside ethos was devolving rapidly, with long-held traditional values challenged by a generation of privileged pseudo-intellectuals.

Vietnam War Protest

America was awash in prolific drug culture, daily protest, and race riots in cities and campuses back home. This anarchy would inflict disorder that eschewed citizens' self-confidence in government entities.

The military inherited this truculent national *hara-kiri* with a vortex of self-destructive behavior that would pervade Marine units. We lost control of cohesiveness, lost our edge, and lost our sense of Corps. Drugs, alcohol, and racial issues became a *force majeure*.

In the bush, Marine units remained a cohesive fighting team. But once back into the rear, they segregated into tribes. Heads and Juicers, Splits and Chucks, Lifers and Short-Timers were frequently doing battle with each other.

Ever-present was the stench of a *bong son bomber* being toked. Heroin and opium were the drugs of choice for those that needed further anesthetization. Hookers, known as *boom boom* girls, were smuggled in red mailbags onto Hill 55.

I refused to get wasted or partake of the merriment, not for any moral reasons or possible disciplinary action; I just needed my senses about me should I hear the call, "Gooks in the wire." After all, we were still at war, and the M-16 still had live rounds in the chamber.

Because we were standing down to go home, Charlie left us alone. They didn't want to do anything to awaken a hell-storm that would come raining down. Marines still had a lot of fight left in them. Besides, we were self-destructing, and nothing the NVA would do could be more harmful than our *suttee*.

In late July 1971, we turned Hill 55 over to the ARVN (Army of the Republic of Vietnam). They took control and

Anti-war Protest

immediately began stripping all the tin off the hooch's and ratfuck anything not cemented down. We moved to Da Nang and didn't look back; *game, set, match*.

Our transportation mode back to San Diego was the Navy ship USS Denver, designated LPD-9 (landing ship, dock) and named after the city, not the singer. The Navy designed the LPD's to transport Marines into battle by sea, using landing crafts and helicopters. Now it transported us back to the world. Having been in the jungle for over twelve months, we weren't even thinking about the stateside battle the USS Denver was transporting us back into. More on that later, but for now, port call!

What a rush! We pulled into Victoria Harbor and, to most of us, the eighth wonder of the modern world, Hong Kong. Beautiful breathtaking skyline, clean, pristine harbor, commercial ships, and cruise liners docked or awaited docking in Hong Kong. Commercial airplanes (not B-52 bombers) were landing and taking off at the airport. The city was alive with people and activity. Beautiful young Asian and European ladies partially dressed in the latest fashion, "Hot Pants."

Hong Kong was a British colony providing essential strategic facilities to the U.S. war effort. Between 1965 and 1971, it ranked among the most prominent destinations for American service members on R&R (rest & relaxation). It frequently was referred to as a haven for tortured souls, but we just called it Adult Disneyland.

I turned twenty in Nam the month before without the opportunity to celebrate my birthday, so a few of my friends and I partied. I could say forever; I had my twentieth birthday party in Hong Kong. Beer, babes, and cricket matches would occupy my week. Double-decker red buses were our primary mode of transportation to plush, clean, expensive restaurants. I would spend six days in an intoxicating fog celebrating. It was a hell of a shindig, from what they told me.

But all good things must end; we waved goodbye to Hong Kong and spent the next eleven days steaming to California.

The arrival was less than celebratory upon docking in San Diego. No *Welcome Home* banners, no loved ones running up and hugging their warriors, no military band playing victory marches. Hell, we weren't expecting a parade, but sneaking into town after dark was creepy.

The ship anchored just after nightfall as the Southern California fog rolled in. The only sounds were the melodic humming of the ship's diesel engines, the annoying grind of the shipyard cranes offloading equipment, and the rhythmic cadence of Marine foot traffic debarking off the boat—a bittersweet homecoming.

We boarded buses and settled in for the ninety-minute ride to Camp Pendleton. Once on base, we moved to Camp Horno, home of the 1st Marine Regiment. We turned our weapons into the armory, drew linen, were assigned a barrack, found a rack, and crashed. That was it, "Welcome Home."

I spent a few days out into the Southern Cal community of restaurants, pubs, and city parks. The anti-military animosity of the locals fringed on out and out deep hatred. It was somewhat expected with all the anti-war sentiments propagating. The My Lai massacre had just hit the news the previous summer; what a shit storm.

In 1968, an Army unit entered the village of My Lai and murdered over 400 unarmed civilians. When the massacre was uncovered and hit the press in 1969, the negative attitudes toward U.S. servicemen got uglier.

Anyone in the military was a baby killer, even the rear echelon Remington Raiders, who were never in the bush or loaded an M-16.

It was easy to pick out a Marine by his haircut, grooming standards, clean shirt, and use of underarm deodorant. The long-haired civilians looked like partyers from Woodstock or homeless derelicts with barbate grooming standards and shabby attire. There was no confusion as to who was in the military.

We were the last primary Marine unit to leave Vietnam. But the Army still had combat forces in-country and would continually sustain causalities. Of course, this was a significant event on the six o'clock national news, breaking headlines of U.S. body count displayed like a basketball scoreboard.

The Journey

There was scattered applause in one pub when Walter Cronkite announced on T.V. that U.S. military deaths for the month totaled 231. Those perverse looks, stares, and attitudes were ubiquitous; *It don't mean nothin'*. I was going home.

As the airplane was touching down in Columbus, Ohio, monomaniacal thoughts raced through my head. *What will she look like? What will I say*? My anxiety grew exponentially. I hadn't seen Karen since I left for Vietnam over a year ago. A few pictures she sent looked nothing like the person I had left.

We initially wrote letters, albeit infrequent at best. After a few months in the bush, I wrote and asked her to stop writing. The red mail bag's arrival without any mail and the constant thoughts of her were weighing heavy on my spirit. Those emotional wastelands distracted me from what I came to Vietnam to do—hunt down and kill bad guys.

Would I recognize her? I felt like I'd changed beyond recognition; I was thinner, having lost almost forty pounds. That can happen with a plebeian diet and walking, continuously walking through the mountains and the jungles of Vietnam, Laos, and Cambodia.

My spirit had also changed. I left, a puerile teen looking for excitement and a need to validate my manhood. I would return with increased temporal maturity. Every problem presented to me would be small compared to a year in the bush. Hell, I survived.

The airport at Port Columbus looked more like a grain storage elevator than an international commercial hub it would later become. The airfield had two runways and a fence to keep the cows from wandering onto the airport proper. The terminal was a single brick building with one baggage collection carousel and a parking lot to accommodate seventy-five cars. No jetway, just steps that abutted the airplane door allowing the passengers to step down onto the tarmac and move directly to the terminal entrance.

The doors opened up into a wide access area that allowed people to walk from the parking lot directly into the terminal and straight to the arrival/departure gates. The building entrance had a section set aside for the rental car agencies and ticket area. The whole concourse was less than a football field in length.

As I took my first step out of the airplane door, I notice two young women on the airport viewing deck, frantically waving. My eyes focused on the blonde lass, attired in a white paisley blouse. As I gave a casual, smiling head nod to the pair of females, their waving and hoopla became more intense. *Was this my homecoming? Was this to be my reward?*

My first thoughts were, *The night air sure is heavier than California, and that young blonde sure is heavier than my pipe dreams.*

I begin to move slowly down the steps onto the tarmac. For some instinctual reason, my moves were slow and deliberate, head down as if I was still walking point in the jungle looking for booby traps. I strolled across the warm tarmac asphalt and walked into the terminal entrance. The two gals on the viewing deck broke visual contact with me and appeared to hurry down to the flight arrival gate. My trepidation grew.

As I warily stepped into the terminal, I saw the two ladies trot through the entrance door. Though they were a good thirty yards from me, I could see the profile of my blonde aspirations. She was not the remembrance of my utopian ladylove, just an average-looking girl with an ugly paisley blouse. As she moved through the terminal, coming even closer, her waving appeared manic, and her steps quickened. I remained slow and deliberate, still looking for that booby trap.

With her rush toward me and our physical distance dwindling, I painfully felt our destinies soon would converge. Her nonathletic pace quickened as her thickset features began exploding in my brain. The classic beauty attributes I remembered— perfect skin and shapely body —were not there.

I replaced the devastating disappointment with a process of how to extricate myself from this *oh shit* moment. I immediately thought up an "arioso" that would be polite and believable as well as harmonious. My critical thinking and military training skills would contrive to pull the ejection handle, find my high school buddies, get drunk, and raise hell. The idea of a sensual reunion was out of the question. The confluence of our two souls just wasn't going to happen.

As she came closer, I suddenly experienced a Vietnam flashback. At that moment, I saw a fragmentation grenade explode with an elegiac effect. Surreal, as if something out of a Jefferson Airplane song. My heartbeat accelerated, the mouth was dry, and my shaking hands were sweaty. I continually assessed the battlefield as the PTSD began to overwhelm me.

Within twenty feet, her vision was demoralizing as the 1968 Vietnam Tet Offensive, or worse, Ohio State losing to Stanford in the 1971 Rose Bowl. Within ten feet of our reunion, I made a command decision; *ABORT, ABORT, ABORT!*

With a broad, asymmetrical smile, this quick-paced blonde reality began to gallop awkwardly toward my citadel. With her welcoming arms extended and plumpish physique entering the kill zone, I took a half step forward and shuffled sideways, bracing myself for the paisley impact.

The plan would be to offer a quick hug, a peck on the cheek, and engage in casual dialogue on the ride home. I would pronounce, "It's not you, it's me. War was hell, and I need time to adjust." With only seconds to spare, I rehearsed this proverbial canned speech.

Then it happened, the gallop didn't slow down, and the extended arms didn't widen to embrace. The paisley-bloused girl ran right by me. *Holly shit!* A tactical error. I had just called in an airstrike on my own position.

After bitch slapping myself back to reality, I did a quick BDA (Bomb Damage Assessment) and reconstituted my plan of attack. So, where was the muse I woolgathered for the last twelve months?

Being a savvy, wily combat veteran, I began thinking of a strategy to ensure I didn't make the same mistake twice. Hell, Charlie couldn't kill me; I wasn't about to get *blown away* in an airport terminal. I needed to develop a solid blueprint for success.

I decided to use the airport paging system to facilitate my ruse. I paged overhead, "Karen Armintrout, please meet your party at the Hertz Rent A Car counter." After the overhead went out a second time, I positioned myself out of sight from the counter. If the next damsel was not a nymphet, I was bolting out of the airport.

I waited, not a few moments, but patiently long enough to see my intended. Then the vision, Erato incarnated. My stargazed memento that was carved into my many sleeps had a promise beyond any expectations.

She wore a perfectly fitting purple jumpsuit emblazed with white flowers. Her young body filled out the fashion in a way only a professional model could. Her beautiful face could launch a thousand ships, or in my case, a thousand M48 Patton Tanks. Her hair was effulgently radiant, perfectly styled with every golden strand in place.

She moved to the designated rendezvous area with grace and flow of the cultured refinement I fell in love with; this was her.

Before I started a move out of my cover and concealment, I needed to make sure it was indeed her. I thought for a moment to drop to my knees and ask God, "Please be this, my destination." But since I had been asking God for too many things during the

The Journey

past twelve months, I decided not to impose and allow him to answer someone else's prayers. I would take my chances.

I moved slowly toward this beauty. Recognition was instant, not only from her ambient grace and splendor but from the look in her eyes, smile on the face, and aura infusing our intended cradling.

We smiled acknowledgment, touched, then hugged, hugged, and hugged again. Unsettled at first, then an unrestrained, soft velvet caress, followed by an impregnable clasping that resembled the tethering of a ship moored in a harbor with the coming of a CAT 4 hurricane. The unspoken outcry, "I'll never let you go," was ever-present.

We spent the next three days and two nights in an impassioned tornadic super twister. We took breaks only to order pizza and dine out at that fine culinary establishment, White Castle. She was it, the real thing.

Since I had two more years on my enlistment, I would have to go back to Camp Pendleton after my leave was up in three weeks. I didn't want any more long separations, so I asked her to live with me in California. She said she wasn't a hippy and would not live with anyone without being married. So, I asked her to marry me. Not very romantic but effective. A month later, we were a young married couple living on the beach in Southern Cal, starting a commitment in figuring out this life contest… fifty years later, *game, set, match, championship.*

Steve Jacklin

Married to my best friend

SHE FELL IN LOVE WITH CRAZY

She didn't know where he would take her
She didn't know if she should go
She didn't know if he would break her
There's only one thing she could know

She didn't think of stormy oceans
She didn't see the glacier melt
She only tasted fresh emotions
She will finally trust herself

She fell in love with crazy
Looking back, she thought would never
Know the feelings of her answer
She fell in love with crazy ... forever

Heartbeats assured her of the plan
Her decision could not be clearer
Just one thing to understand
End of innocents was drawing nearer

She fell in love with crazy
Looking back, she thought she'd never
understand the feelings of her answer
She fell in love with crazy ... forever

He made her smile... Just like a child
He made the angry world seem clean
Occasionally, she could see
and believe her world's serene

Flight Wings

Chapter 5
I AM NOW A MARINE PILOT (Part 1) —
"HELICOPTERS DON'T FLY, THEY JUST BEAT THE AIR INTO SUBMISSION"

T-34 Mentor

Reflection, Pensacola, Florida, 1979. Naval Flight School was difficult, but I made it. The day I received my aviator wings was a sentinel moment in my life. Not as important as marriage or kids, but close to being my professional apex. The golden wings fitted proudly above my left breast pocket on my uniform. I was now a member of an exclusive club.

Funny how I landed there. I was a twenty-four-year-old senior in college sitting in the student center bullshitting with other football players. Our discussions ranged from graduation to life after graduation to deep spiritual mentation like, *Who invented soap on the rope*? Two Marine staff sergeants entered through the main door during our collegial forum and moved briskly to our table. They were on a recruiting mission looking for candidates to become Marine Corps Officers.

As they moved to our table, their focus seemed to lock in on me like a TOW missile engaging a North Vietnamese BTR-60. After the recruiter's customary presentment, the Marine staff sergeants began a series of questions, focused mainly in my direction, hell-bent on pitching the opportunities of me wearing the eagle, globe, and anchor.

As they began their presentation, the first question directed at me was, "Do you want to learn how to lead men?" They had no idea of my Marine Corps antecedent and having led men in Vietnam. To them, I was just another college jock, albeit a little older, at an expensive school. I politely gave them a "No, thank you." Their second question was, "Would you be interested in graduate school? We have a law program we can get you into after you finish undergrad." I politely declined, explaining I had grad school plans and was going to Ohio State's School of Allied Medicine with intentions of becoming a physical therapist.

And then, *SATORI*, as if enlightenment coming from the mouth of Buddha. The Marine recruiters began, "We have an aviation program. Would you like to be a Marine Pilot?" I wasn't like some kids, dreaming about planes, wanting to land on aircraft carriers, or strapped into a cockpit with a thousand gallons of explosive jet fuel underneath my butt. Being a pilot never crossed my mind.

But there it was, the payola! A leather flight jacket and aviator sunglasses. The next thing I knew, I signed the papers, and the Marines were paying for my private flight lessons at Ohio State University. I was on my way to being a pilot, with a few stops, of course, along the route; graduation, ten weeks of OCS (Officer Boot Camp), six months of TBS (The Basic School), then two years in Pensacola for flight training.

The training wasn't particularly hard, and I had an instinct for the 3D aerial environment. I also was a quick study and could multi-task, all traits needed to complete flight training. But the aircraft scheduling was problematic.

The Naval Flight Command had transitioned from the T-28 Trojan flight training aircraft to the T-34 Mentor training airplane. The Mentor would have all kinds of flight problems that would delay or cancel training. I was like a finely tuned athlete, mentally ready for the game but postponed due to the stadium lights not working or some dumb ass kneeling for the national anthem and delaying the kickoff. It threw off the momentum and rhythm, but I adjusted.

The student pilots had a macabre sense of humor that bordered on insensitivity and callousness. Having been to combat, I saw the same gallows humor in the jungles of Vietnam. My psychology 101 class would define this as sublimation, displacement, and repression. I called it college fraternity humor and locker room hilarity.

A few of the frequent dirges recited were "News today from VT-3, your son just flew into a tree." VT-3 was the fixed-wing training squadron all-new pilot trainees would go through. Another lament was "A successful flight was when the landings equaled the takeoffs."

After arriving at flight training with his new wife, a good friend of mine passed through Pensacola's main gate and added to this wordplay. Inside the entryway to the Naval Air Training Command was Barrancas National Cemetery. The wife asked in all seriousness, "Why all the graves?" With a serious tone and sobering reply, my friend answered, "Honey, those are flight students that crashed during training." Two weeks later, the missus discovered the true purpose of the gravestones in the cemetery. Bill was quite the jokester, in line with the rest of us satirists and in the dog house for few days.

In August 1979, I was *winged* and on my way to my first duty station, MCAS New River, Jacksonville, North Carolina, to fly UH-1N Huey Helicopters. I looked forward to the Huey because of stories I heard about its single ship mission and the cool places the mission took the pilots. After six years of "beating the air into submission" flying Huey's, I was not disappointed. From Norway to Israel, from Denmark to Lebanon, I compiled frequent flyer miles doing the Huey missions, seeing some fascinating places, and experiencing many exciting happenings.

HT8 Helo Traning Squadron

Early in my Marine helicopter career, I was part of military operations in Norway. In the early 1980s, the squadron would fly aboard a Navy amphibious assault ship and sail to Northern Norway. We deployed for three months, playing in the snow and flying the Norwegian fjords. We did our flying 75 miles north of the Arctic Circle at a NATO air station called Bardufoss, 45 miles south of Tromso, Norway. Our squadron commander worked out a good deal for us. He secured billeting at a lodge in Andselv, a small community adjacent to the Air Station. We housed officers on the hill and enlisted in a lodge at the bottom of the hill. Every other evening, a truck would arrive with cases of duty-free beer for the officers and enlisted. Always take care of your troops.

Duty-free was a term meaning no taxes. The tariff could be as high as $4 on a bottle of beer. The Brits, who were authorized duty-free, would sell us the beer for fifty cents a bottle. We'd sell it to the lodge owner for seventy-five cents a bottle. He would then charge us a dollar for the same bottle of beer. Not sure how this worked out or who was keeping track of the funds. After a hard day of flying, *keeping the world safe for democracy*, we didn't care about the auditing just so the GullMack beer kept flowing. Later in life, I would presume Arthur Anderson used this practice in their Enron accounting.

So how did I end up in a Norwegian lodge drinking Mack and flying the fjords? It started by landing on the USS Guam off Morehead City, NC, then transiting two weeks across the Atlantic, steaming into the English Channel, and finally into the North Sea. Along the way, a few things happened, like the *emergency leave saga*.

Narvik Norway

We had a flight of two Huey's taking military personnel ashore on emergency leave to Mildenhall, England, a joint Royal Air Force, and civilian use airport. Mildenhall was located a few hundred miles northwest of London. The U.S. had fighter jets stationed on the Brit base and had regular U.S. transport and civilian aircraft flying back to the States. Our passengers on emergency leave would get further transportation home at Mildenhall.

The weather over the Channel was perfect as the two aircraft took off. But the USS Guam's surface radar was down, and the ship had no clue within 100 miles where we were when launched, just somewhere in the English Channel. We planned to hit the coast, pick up a recognizable terrain feature, get our bearings, and continue our mission. Note: in the 1980s, Marine tactical helicopters were equipped with only TACAN, VOR, and

DME. LORAN and GPS systems were being developed for aviation but not yet used in tactical helicopters.

As we approached the English coast, a wall of fog blanketed the cliffs keeping us from any reference point on the ground and continuing inland. We could have been anywhere along the Solent between the coast of Hampshire and the Isle of Wight. We circled for thirty minutes without success. With an hour flight in front of us, our fuel became an issue, so I contacted a British Nimrod patrol aircraft on a universal radio frequency. Our radio call requested the patrol aircraft to relay to ATC (Air Traffic Control) our need for an instrument clearance through the fog.

Norway 1982 FlyingUH-1N Huey

After contact with ATC, the Nimrod requested our current position. Since the USS Guam didn't know where we were when launched and with the coast obscured by fog, no one else in the flight could identify our exact position. I said, *hell with this crap*, we needed a ground reference point, so I made a command decision. I landed in an English pasture and handed my crew chief a map. He exited the aircraft, sauntered over to a Brit farmer, who was tending his cows, and asked where we were on the map. The intrigued farmer grinned, pointed to a spot on the map, and the chief crew returned to the noisy helicopter. As we took off, the dairy herd seemed impervious to the green metal interloper.

We now had our fix on the ground, and I contacted the Nimrod with our position, who relayed to ATC, who gave us our clearance. We did an instrument climb through the fog, and it was clear at 4500 feet, *VFR on Top*. We continued to Mildenhall, landed, and successfully delivered our passengers for their flight back home. Right out of the military handbook FM 1369, with the title, *How to Make Shit Happen*, mission complete.

We closed out our flight plan and checked into billeting for our rooms. Then we went to the Officer's Club for a meal and a quiet evening. Unfortunately, four Air Force pilots would disrupt the anticipated evening calm.

After approaching our dinner table and a cursory greeting, they suggested that we join them in the bar for a game of Crud after our meal. The game is a fast-paced recreational pastime loosely based on billiards and originating in the Royal Canadian Air Force. The U.S. Air Force pilots had adopted it as their official game to showcase their superior athletic fitness and prowess. We were sure the games gentlemen rules had long ago been established. Still, every time Marines would enter an Air Force Officer's Club, the Air Force Jocks wanted to play Crud with modified rules, albeit more aggressive and less collegial. Hockey body checks and thrown elbows were the norms, degenerating into body slams, full nelsons, and chock holds.

Before the night was over, an Air Force Pilot was under the pool table, either passed out drunk or knocked unconscious. In the corner was a Marine pilot and Air Force F-15 driver engaged in a Roman-Greco wrestling match culminating in a hammerlock and an Air Force submission. We suffered our wounds and battle scars too, but the damage was minimal. The Officers Club would sustain significantly more battle wounds.

The club manager entered the arena and abruptly asked us to leave. I later heard an official report from the base commander was sent to the Naval attaché in England requesting payment for the club's damages. It wasn't going to be the first official report on this trip.

The following day, we did our preflight routine for the planned trip back to the English Channel. The weather was crappy, with low visibility and ceiling. We opted to take the flight to 5500 feet above the clouds with a planned heading that could take us back to the USS Guam. We started our engines, did a final fuel check, and taxied out to the duty runway.

In front of us was a German Lufthansa commercial airliner. It was holding short of the duty runway, obviously not ready for takeoff. We were burning a shit load of fuel, waiting behind the plane for his departure.

After a fifteen-minute wait, the airport control tower, with a slightly agitated tone, radioed the Lufthansa aircraft, "Flight 734, say the reason for delay". The pilot from Lufthansa Flight 734, with a slight German accent, radioed back, "We're looking for a passenger." As it would happen, someone radioed back and told the German pilot to, "Check the oven." Holy Crap! This quip had the makings of an international incident.

We never knew who transmitted this facetious repartee but knew it didn't come from the Huey bubbas. We got nailed for it anyway. The Lufthansa captain would not take off until he received an official apology from the control tower.

After burning up additional twenty minutes of fuel, we were cleared for takeoff and were soon out of Mildenhall's air space. We were sure the shit would hit the fan with this episode and probably get back to the ship before we would, and it did. Our injudicious forays provoked the Commodore's tirade, "Those damn Huey's are grounded."

The drama wasn't over. We climbed to 5500 feet and recalibrated our ground speed and fuel burn rate. No surprise, with an 80-knot headwind, reserve JP-5 would be skoosh with *BINGO* (minimum) fuel once we hit the Channel. Upon reaching the coast, that would leave us less than twenty minutes of fuel until *SPLASH*. A wet landing in the English Channel if we couldn't find the ship.

Before takeoff, the weatherman gave us a ceiling of 800 feet for transit back to the English Channel. As such, we decided to descend at or below 800 feet, where the winds were more advantageous to our ground speed and fuel consumption.

We requested and received an ATC clearance to descend out of 5500 feet. Passing through 800 feet, we were still popeye (in the clouds). We finally broke out at just below 500 feet above the ground. We decided this would be our planned cruising altitude back to the English Channel.

We reported to ATC, "Level at 500 feet," and canceled our instrument flight plan. We continued with visual flight rules. Our altitude would fluctuate between 300 and 800 feet above the ground for the next forty-five minutes, occasionally flying over an English hamlet at the lower altitude. I'm sure the rotor blades' vibration caused windows to shake and the awakening of milady.

On our low-level incursion, we suddenly came upon a national artifact that surprised us and had the potential to cause further consternation with Navy brass on the flagship.

The focus of our revelation was the gathering of stones that came under the nose of our flight path. Due to the low ceiling (approximately 350 feet above the ground) and low visibility (less than a quarter of a mile), we couldn't pinpoint our exact location over the ground. As we looked over our aircraft's nose, there was *STONEHENGE*. Even with an aggressive "yank and bank" maneuver to avoid the site, our flight path still took us over the right half of the ancient dolmens.

Holy crap! I was sure the possibility of our rotor wash dislodging any of the Neolithic 3000-year-old stones was remote. Still, the required fly-over altitude for any British cultural icon was 1500 feet above the ground, not 300 feet.

Our saving grace was no tourist traffic visiting the standing ring of bluestones or any Druids performing human sacrifices on the Santonian Seafold Chalk. We got lucky with this one. No one sent any complaints to the flagship about our *faux pa*. Our errant detour was known only to four Marine pilots and Morrigu, the Celtic god of war.

We continued on our flight over the Plains of Hastings and East Sussex. We landed on the USS Guam two hours later and experienced the expected uncomfortable ass-chewing with the Commodore repeating his earlier comments about Huey's being grounded. This prohibition would pass, and we were back in the cockpit two days later. As a Tom Petty song goes, *It's Good to be King*.

We had three successful months of flying in the artic. After finishing the operation, we left the Norwegian base, packed our aircraft stuff, and flew back aboard the ship. We spent five days steaming to Southern England, where we had a port call in Portsmouth, 70 miles southwest of London, and home to the Royal Navy.

We did the usual tourist stuff, visit the HMS Victory, flagship to Vice-Admiral Horatio Nelson, and some sightseeing in London. On our last day of port call in Portsmouth, we visited the famous Nelson Pub to extol our exploits in Norway and acclaim what great pilots we were. Of course, there was plenty of Guinness Stout imbibed that would amplify our aerial greatness.

Known facts about Brit beer, it had no carbonation and is served at room temperature. It goes down smooth, not filling. No buzz with the first four pints chugged. You then turn to your friend and mumble, "This shit doesn't have any effect on me." Moments later, your eyes cross, your head spins, and words came out of your mouth pixelated. Never underestimate the power of a good British Stout.

On one occasion, two other Marine pilots and I were sitting in a booth at Nelsons Pub with three Brit Airmen. We had just finished a joint operation in Norway with them on the English aircraft carrier Hermes. The Brit pilots at our table couldn't outfly us but could differently out bullshit us. The stories became more aggrandized the more Guinness Stout we hammered down.

A Brit pilot named Andy sat right next to me. He and I were the unofficial captains of the us-versus-them teams debating (really drunken arguments) over aircraft tactics, maneuvers, and the better helicopter—the Marine UH-1N Huey or the British WG-13 Lynx.

The debate was contentious with the preverbal high five when either side scored a verbal jousting point. The climate returned to a jocular airing when someone at the table would order another round of Guinness. We went through these Don Quixote iterations for over an hour, with each pilot telling tales of their glory in battling windmills. The twenty-something Andy relished in these intermural games and seemed to buy most of the rounds.

As we began another segment of *who had more of the right stuff*, my commanding officer entered the front door of Nelson's Pub. He noticed the six of us sitting in the booth and moved to our table. He gave the usual salutation, "Hello Jackal, how are you?"

Before I could return the customary perfunctory, "Fine, sir," he snapped to attention. Then turned to the occupant on my left and gave a "Good evening sir, hope all my pilots are behaving themselves."

Andy responded, "They certainly are Colonel, have a good evening," seemingly dismissing my boss.

My commanding officer abruptly turned and walked out of Nelson's Pub.

Andy had a shit-eating grin on his face, and I sat momentarily bewildered. I looked across the table as the other

Brits were laughing their asses off. I asked one of Andy's companions, "What the fuck was that about."

The Brit pointed to the man sitting next to me and said, "Jackal, let me introduce to you your royal highness Prince Andrew, the Duke of York."

No screaming eagle shit! So, the man I had just spent the last two hours with, throwing down Guinness Stout and exchanging insults, was at the time second in the line of succession to the throne of England. At that point, I noticed (or finally paid attention to) the Princes' security detail, two inside at the front and back door and two outside on the street.

Discretion and protocol would demand that I politely excuse myself, gather up my two cohorts, and leave the table. But having drunk enough liquid courage and finding the episode pants pissing hilarious, I opted to continue this shindig. I turned to the Duke of York and irreverently said, "Andy, you gonna buy another round of drinks?"

"Jammy! Another round on the Queen," he accommodated jubilantly.

We spend another forty-five minutes getting further liquored up, yakking about who could outfly who and who had *more of the right stuff*.

Andy and my paths didn't cross again while in Portsmouth. As we were getting ready to pull out of port, The British Defense Ministry ordered an English task force to the Falklands Islands, a Brit territory. The conflict was a 10-week undeclared war after Argentina invaded and occupied the islands. Over 600 Argentine military personnel, 255 British military personnel, and three Falkland Islanders died during hostilities, lots of rockets, lots of bullets, lots of bombs during the 74-day campaign.

During the conflict, Andy, The Duke of York, second in line to the throne of England, flew numerous combat missions and was heroically aggressive. He was highly decorated and would prove that he did have *more of the right stuff*. Ballsy dude!

THE EXIT SIGN

Let the fire continue as the smoke remains aloft
Let the amber glow as the mannequin remarks
The ashes that are left untilled are blown away with wind
Leave us all when mornings come, personage again

Times are spent with happenstance and dreams inside the realm
Nothing changes what has been, with who is at the helm
Guiding past the marble vase, the violent storm that builds
Then chasing down the harsh resound, later hear unwilled

Say what must and speak not long, to what is forward bent
Heedless wrangle, endless loops, dilute what noises meant
If there's a change in advance to liquidate the rage
The book is done so to some, continue to turn the page

Whatever path is taken, whatever roads are cruised
Whatever time has given, if only what was used
All that sanguinely brings, by the sweetness of the wine
Or down the hall, through the squall, to the exit sign

Shipboard OPS

Chapter 6
I AM NOW A MARINE PILOT (Part 2) - *"FLY IT TILL THE LAST PIECE STOP MOVING"*

After my Norwegian sojourns in 1982, the squadron scheduled me to take two Huey's aboard the USS Inchon as part of an MAU (Marine Amphibious Unit). This entity type was a task-organized combat unit with an assortment of helicopters and twelve hundred highly trained Marines. We loaded the ship on the East Coast and spent two weeks floating toward the Mediterranean Sea. Once in the Med, we would conduct any mission the Pentagon assigned.

Before entering the Med, the MAU scheduled a training mission with the Danish Military in southern Denmark. The flying would prove to be challenging, testing all our aeronautical skills and aviation talent. But on one such occasion, the story had more to do with an ill-fated land-based operation than any aerial prowess.

Marine Amphibious Unit

We landed at the Danish Air Force base for a preliminary planning session. After the meeting with the Dane pilots, we all adjourned to the officers club for a post-planning session. Yeah, officers club. Were you expecting pilots to fraternize at a Danish coffee house eating pastries?

The Tuborg and Heineken were flowing oft and in more than sufficient quantity. The Dane pilots made it a point to prove their Scandinavian drinking prowess over us. Of course, we took the bait and tried to keep up with them—our first mistake.

The second mistake we made was not calling a ride to take us back to our quarters for the evening. After a few hours of festive comradery with our hosts, we five Marines decided to leave the pub and take the quarter-mile walk back to our tents.

Somewhere along the way, the hump became too laborious for my buddy Goose and me. Our other three comrades kept walking out of sight as we took a break on a stone ledge. We pondered our situation and decided we could easily stumble back to camp. After a few moments into our intoxicated promenade, it became apparent we weren't capable of any further foot travels.

Then we saw it, a Danish government van. It looked like the vehicle was parked for the night, welcoming us to utilize its back seats as a nocturnal boudoir. We wandered to the side of the van, opened the door, and climbed in to sleep off our earlier revelries. We had a decent night's sleep, with minimal disquietude.

At dawn light, I was awakened by a startled expletive, then "Hey Jackal, someone came over to the window, looked in, and knocked," Goose whispered in a quiet yet frantic tone. Being slightly in control of my mental faculties, I immediately had what I thought was a flash of brilliance. I blathered in a soft, somewhat coherent mumble, "Goose, on the count of three, we'll both pop up. If anyone sees or says anything to us, we'll say we asked someone for a ride, and they said sure, wait in the van." Hell, it was worth a try.

We arose from our horizontal posture on the count of three and were surprised, almost wetting our flight suits. We had been sleeping in the Danish Generals Command Van. I smelled an international incident.

The Journey

We slowly moved out of the vehicle, quietly securing the doors and head-nodding to a couple of Danish soldiers a few yards away. They were surprised to see us. We were even more surprised to recognize that we were parked in front of the Danish headquarters building with a huge general officer's three-star flag attached to the flagpole.

We started walking to the main road, acting as if we were supposed to be there. Three things gave us confidence as to our prevarication. One, the Dane soldiers looking at us spoke broken English. "Keep a smile on your face and speak in a tone that sounds like you know what you're talking about," was my advice to Goose.

The second thing that gave us cover was we knew this was a NATO practice operation; no live bullets.

And the third factor, these were Danes, not Norwegians. We would have gotten our asses kicked by Bjon or Gunnar before they let us go if we were in Norway. No worry about any physical confrontation with these Danish stoners.

Once on the road, we flagged down a military jeep driven by a Marine private. We told the Marine we needed immediate transportation back to the airfield for a Level One Launch with the Danish Air Force. There was no such thing as a Level One Launch, but it impressed the driver enough for him to deviate from his route and transport us back to our aircraft. It certainly wasn't two hungover Marine Captains smelling like Tuborg that caused the Marine driver to reroute his morning trip ticket.

Fifteen minutes later, we were dropped off at our Huey, thanked the driver for the ride, identified ourselves as Captain John Holmes and Captain Ron Jeremy. He drove away, feeling good, having just ensured a Level One Launch.

We grabbed our sleeping bags from under the back seats of our Huey and crashed. Lesson learned from this episode, don't try to outdrink Danish pilots.

The next scheduled stop for the fleet was a port call in France. Unfortunately, our *Champs-Élysées* party was preempted by the June 1982 Israeli incursion into Lebanon.

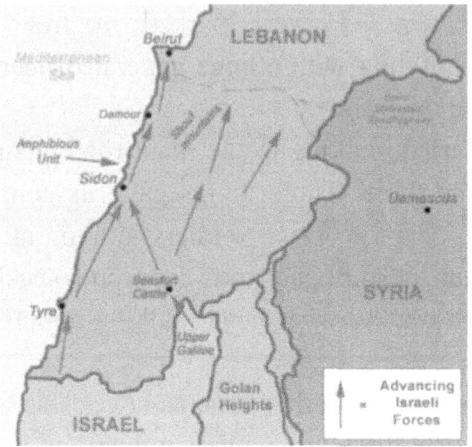

1982 Israeli Advance into Lebanon

After the IDF (Israeli Defense Force) planned a twenty-mile invasion into Southern Lebanon to provide a security buffer, Israeli Defense Minister Ariel Sharon expanded the operation and went all the way to Beirut's suburbs. The strategic purpose was to eliminate the PLO's (Palestinian Liberation Organization) threat to Northern Israel.

The PLO would continually launch rockets from Southern Lebanon into Israeli villages, killing and wounding civilians. They would attack small towns with the intent of killing as many Jews as they could.

On one such killing spree, a team of PLO assassins crossed the border and occupied an Israeli grade school in Ma'alot. They took 115 Israeli hostages, including 105 children. Before the standoff was finished, the assassins had murdered 22 Israeli school kids. The Lebanese invasion became Sharon's *casus belli,* a preventive move to promote security in Northern Israeli.

The history of the PLO was scarred with chaos, violence, and displacement.

In September 1970, after trying a coup d'état against the Jordanian Monarchy, the PLO was expelled from Jordan. Over 6000 refugees ended up in Lebanon, where they promoted turbulence and incited the Lebanese Civil War in 1975.

Beirut Lebanon

Beirut, the Paris of the Middle East's, had become a shit hole during the sectarian war, Maronite Christians fighting the PLO. Massacres among women and children were a regular occurrence during the 15-year conflict. One such bloodbath brought the Marines to Beirut.

In September of 1982, the Christian Phalange fighters entered the Palestinian refugee camps of Sabra and Shatila. Before the night was over, over 3000 Muslim women and children had been murdered by the Christian rampage. The Phalange justified the killing as a reprisal for over 1000 Christian women and children massacred by the PLO in the Lebanese town of Damour earlier in the civil war. This *Dar al-Harb* (House of War) was where the Pentagon translocated the 26th Marine Amphibious Unit. Refereeing an untenable peace was now our mission, no screaming eagle shit.

We moved the squadron ashore and took up residence in tents we erected at BIA (Beirut International Airport), at one time the busiest and most beautiful airport in the Middle East. Now it was a bombed-out wreck with destroyed aircraft and vehicles covering the cratered runways and fragmented tarmac. The years of fighting had demolished the airport's terminal and control tower. This destructive carnage would be our new home for the next six months.

Beirut Airport

The first flight I took from BIA blew my mind. I lifted off from our airport LZ (Landing Zone) to transition to the south toward northern Israel. At midfield, lined up like cords of wood, were over 600 bodies wrapped in Muslim white burial shroud. The corpses were from the earlier killings at the refugee camps.

The corpses had been positioned along the airport taxiway, awaiting further air transportation somewhere for eventual burial. Before leaving air traffic control, I murmured to my copilot, "These people are bat shit crazy," then checked out with our base operations. I put the body carnage behind me and casually cruised southwest as if on my way to a beach resort—just another day at the office.

I continued my flight south to northern Israel, landing in a town called Kiryat Shmona. At least three times a week, I transported American diplomats to this location. They were from the U.S. State Department to help broker a cease-fire and Israeli troop withdrawal for Lebanon. For three months, negotiators would hold peace talks in this northern Israeli town. The talks had a snowball chance in Sinai of being successful.

Once we dropped off Ambassador Moe Draper and his delegation for the scheduled talks, we were without a purpose for the next twelve hours except to wait for the meeting to adjourn and return the diplomatic team to Beirut airport. As a result of this downtime, we did some major sightseeing, Golan Heights, the

Hula Valley, Sea of Galilee, Mt Hermon. One such *tourist de jour* was a trip to Jerusalem and Bethlehem during the Christmas season; this was, without a doubt, the highlight of my years of many travels.

Whenever I would arrive in a new area or country, I would read everything I could about the people, culture, and history. I would also pick up a few phrases of the local language to facilitate getting around. Terms like, "where's the restaurant," or "how much is the bus ticket," or more valuable a saying, "two draft beers please."

Like Islam and the Hajj, I think all Christians should make a trip to the Holy Land. The journey was informative, emotional, and spiritually complete. Walking through Via Dolorosa or quietly meandering by the Sea of Galilee would engulf the spirit with a holy passion. Suggestion, pawn your firstborn if need be, but purchase the ticket and schedule the trip.

As we were preparing to leave the Eastern Med, we had one more flight to Israel. A CH-53 (Shitter) flew along to carry supplies needed by the U.S. Embassy in Tel Aviv. We landed at Sde Dov Airport, just outside Tel Aviv, and proceeded to the Sheridan Hotel to check in. We arrived at 10:30 in the morning, with check-in time at 2:00 in the afternoon. We decided to take care of our business at the Embassy and return to check-in.

The six of us left the hotel lobby and walked the four blocks to the U.S. Embassy. We reported in with the Marine guard and went to the FSO (Foreign Service Officer) in charge of logistics. After delivering our package, paperwork signing, and discussing what's next, we left the Embassy.

Before heading back to the Sheridan, we decided to grab some chow at a Hungarian restaurant. Lunch was great, goulash with beef paprika served over tarhonya. Our walk back was slow and casual, with the usual pilot "bull shit" comradery.

As we approached the hotel, we noticed an Israeli bomb squad inspecting a brown backpack lying against a six-foot retaining wall adjacent to the hotel entrance. We stayed a clear distance from the activity but close enough to check out all the action. The bomb squad seemed to huddle, deciding what to do next.

Then as if on cue, the officers spread out, and one team member uncased a high-powered rifle. He then aimed the gun at the backpack and fired. The discharging of the weapon caused an ear-piercing sound that generated a burst of audible laughter and a "what the hell just happened" from our group.

Within a minute, clarity arrived. Rudy, a Shitter pilot, began to screech, "That's my backpack; they just shot my backpack." It seemed the dumb ass had left his backpack in the Sheridan lobby when we went to the Embassy. A sign in the hotel lobby read, NO UNATTENDED BAGS PERMITTED.

This unattended bag became suspicious, and hotel security called the bomb squad. They used a robot to reposition the bag outside against the six-foot retaining wall. As the bomb squad decided their next move, the SWAT captain heard a faint motorized sound coming from the tote. The decision was made, shoot and kill the backpack.

A brand new $800 Nikon camera was inside the satchel. With all the backpack jostling, the camera's automatic focus device activated, causing a motorized sound. The bomb squad commander decided to neutralize the threat without knowing the cause of the noise or possible danger inside the haversack.

A few moments after the fatal shot, a bomb technician approached the backpack, opened it, and began laying out the rucksack's contents on the sidewalk. There it was, killed in action, Rudy's new Nikon.

The shot into the backpack hit the camera dead center, shattering the photographic nemesis into more than a few pieces.

"They shot my camera; they shot my camera," was repeatedly heard as the five of us, amused, walked into the hotel, leaving Rudy behind to explain to an enraged Israeli policeman why he left his bag in the hotel lobby unattended. For us, just another day at the office.

After another Marine unit replaced our squadron, and we started out of the Eastern Mediterranean and back to the states. I left with lifetime memories of the Holy Land and an eerie sense of foreboding.

The Middle East was complete with car bombs and suicide attacks. I had a rudimentary understanding of these tactics and was surprised the head shed did not take the possibility seriously. It wasn't rocket surgery.

The political wing of our Lebanon mission seemed more obsessed with public relations than tactical security. Sentries were not allowed to have rounds chambered in their M-16's, should they have an accidental discharge and shoot a civilian. I'm sure the State Department, not DOD, drove this insane policy.

My premonition of horror would become a reality with over 241 Marines and Sailors' death in October 1983.

The voyage back home was uneventful, except for the Moroccan Airport incident.

In the early 1980s, most Marine tactical aircraft did not have the state-of-the-art navigation systems that we have today. The ADF, automatic direction finder, VOR, TACAN, and map reading were the primary means of navigating. Most TACAN's also had a mileage indicator called DME used for arching. A DME arc is an imaginary circle, defined by a DME distance from the VOR. A DME arc involves flying a circular course around a VOR/DME or VORTAC station at a specified distance.

Simply put, fix a point on your TACAN. If the mileage decreases, you're getting closer to the station. If the mileage increases, you're moving away from the station. Note: the mileage indicator was not a LED but an old analog rotating mileage device, similar to an odometer in a car. This mileage indicator was the machine that almost caused an international airspace violation.

We had a mission to take an advance party to Rota, Spain, to prepare for the squadron's arrival. After launching from the USS Guam in the Western Mediterranean, we pinpointed our position south of Almeria Spain. The weather deteriorated, with the visibility dropping to less than 2 miles and the ceiling coming down to 500 feet. We planned for a direct flight through Gibraltar to Rota.

Unfortunately, the Spaniards refused the clearance due to the English still owning and possessing the Rock. Gibraltar's British sovereignty was formalized with a treaty in 1713, with Gibraltar becoming a British colony in 1830. The Brits still owned Gibraltar in 1983, and the angry Spaniards refused to allow any flights into their country that either originated or navigated through Gibraltar.

Our backup plan was to circumnavigate over water through the Straits of Gibraltar by using our DME arch around the British Oversea Territory and approach Spain from the Atlantic side. We estimated the Straits to be 10 miles across. An 8-mile arch would keep us clear of Gibraltar to the north with enough distance from Morocco to our south. Sounds like the perfect plan, not quite.

As we approached the Rock and began our arching, the visibility dropped to less than 1/4 mile. We maintained a 500 feet altitude and were quite comfortable flying over the water, keeping our distance from Gibraltar. Abeam the halfway point through the Straits, my left seated copilot casually remarked, "Hey Jackal, should we be flying over land?"

Oops! It seemed our DME arch was a mile off, and we were now flying over the Moroccan Tanger-Boukhalef Airport, a major international airfield in Tangier, Morocco.

The Journey

After a quick *WTF*, we made a sharp turn to the north, and once over water, we continued on our way, albeit a much smaller arch.

Forty minutes later, we arrived at Rota Spain with no complaints, no harm, and no foul with our Vasco De Gama's rhumba-line navigation technique.

After a week in Rota, turning over equipment and classified material to our fleet replacement, we started our 10-day voyage home. The excitement of seeing family, being back on dry land, and watching Mark Knopfler and Dire Straits on MTV was powerful.

Keep flying till the parts stop moving

This reunion with loved ones would always be as if you had met anew, regardless of how long you were gone or how many times you would travel. A transition period would also be required once back at home base. The reprogramming would start after pulling anchor out of Rota.

The first thing was to clean up our language and reprogram our testosterone-filled attitudes. No more "F" bombs or profanity-laced diatribes. Telling your children, "Pick up your fucking shoes, or I'll kick our behind," was now revised to a kindler, "Please remove your shoes from the living room, or we may have a further conversation."

We had to replace the explosive son of a bitch, god damn, and holy shit with, wow, that's terrible, goodness gracious, and crapola. After eight months at sea, we needed the whole ten-day period for a transition, similar to a reprogramming session in a North Korean reeducation camp.

The second thing that needed retooling was who's now in charge. An obvious fact, but often not always in line with your hubris. Having spent your last eight months in charge with expectations of continuing to be in charge when home, it was often overlooked that your wife had also been in charge. She ran the household and daily solved family issues. The last thing she, and the family, needed was for you to come into their house and start barking orders.

The squadron chaplain would give us coming home lectures on what to expect, what not to expect, and what not to do. For those of us who took it seriously, the classes were needed schooling.

After ten days of steaming across the Atlantic, we had the East Coast insight. The next morning, we started our aircraft and launched toward the North Carolina shoreline.

Checking in with the New River Air Station control tower were twenty-one Marine helicopters in formation, requesting permission to land at the squadron area. I'm sure the sight of the inbound aircraft was impressive for the families awaiting our arrival. For us, the view of dry land and home was electrifying.

Within ten miles of the airfield, the lead aircraft radioed "New River Tower, a flight of twenty-one inbound for landing." The tower responded, "Roger, clear to land, welcome home."

Once landed and shut down, the Marines identified their loved ones amongst the crowd of well-wishers. Some reunions were reassuring, few were passionate, but most familial unifications were punctuated with awkward hugs, clumsy kisses, and meaningless chatter. It would take time to get reacquainted.

Aside from the happy homecomings, at least one squadron mate, who had a wife and family eight months earlier, now had no one to awkwardly hug or participate in meaningless chatter with. He had a family no more. With lengthy separation, this was the price he paid to be a Marine.

After the families and aircrew cleared the tarmac, the real reason for the stop in Rota, Spain, became apparent.

A forklift moved toward the CH-53's, the ramps came down, and the forklift got busy unloading pallets of fine wine, expensive China, and other booty.

Rota was a duty-free zone (no tax) with inexpensive items. The only thing that controlled our purchases was the ability for the CH-53 to transport it back to Stateside. The offloading and staging of the pallets on the tarmac resembled the Mongol's Golden Horde bringing back copious bounty to Mongolia after sacking Kyiv.

With what seemed to be a short stay at home, the Marines, like the Mongols, would saddle up and again ride toward battle, surviving on a diet of horse blood and liquor, figuratively speaking, of course.

TRAVELING MINSTREL SHOW

She was the daughter of a Traveling Minstrel Show
Players had performances ... always had to go
They'd return a happy lot... egos satisfied
Hide inside the status quo, but then they realized
The time they spent away from her could never be replaced
Promises they gave ... the look upon her face
When they sat her on their lap and sang a song or two
The tears would fill the eyes and blind the music coming through

Steve Jacklin

Again they sailed and traveled out with the seventh fleet
Masters of their destiny or so they liked to think
Changing course a couple times... the water it got rough
They threw the captain overboard and danced upon the roof
When the bosses heard of this, their tempers became enraged
They looked for scapegoats everywhere but had no one to shame
Searching close to home... that is where they found
Stripped for everyone to see and kneeling on the ground

She turned and sang to the crowd, "are you proud now"
She cried and cried and cried, "are you proud now"
She wouldn't let it die now "are you proud now"

Told her "we would make you proud to be a part of this"
All you do is take the blame... absorb a couple hits
She said she would be the one to promulgate the lies
If Pilot needs a Jesus Christ that he can crucify
Gladly she would face the facts because she remembers well
The times they put her on their laps and had some songs to sell

She turned and sang to the crowd, "are you proud now"
She cried and cried and cried "are you proud now"
She wouldn't let it die now "are you proud now"

Old and gray the minstrel show has played its final hit
In Lebanon, they sang and sung before they finally quit
They traveled home and tried in vain to catchup twenty years
They were shocked to realize... she had no more tears

The Journey

Special OPS

Chapter 7
SPECIAL OPERATIONS - *"FINAGLE'S LAW OF DYNAMIC NEGATIVES."*

Reflection, August 1983: I'm out of the cockpit for eighteen months. After my Mediterranean deployment, I volunteered for duty with 2nd ANGLICO (Air, Naval Gunfire, Liaison, Company), a special operations unit for Marines pilots to be attached to the Army's 82nd Airborne Division or Ranger Battalion.

The ANGLICO Marines' job was to act as a FAC (Forward Air Controller) directing Navy and Marine aircraft strikes or utilize naval gunfire from offshore ships when needed by the Army. This assignment was a highlight in my officer career.

All the ANGLICO Marines were parachute qualified. This qualification required a three-week course at the Army's Airborne School (Jump School) at Fort Benning, Georgia. The Commanding Officer of ANGLICO wanted to ensure his Marines sent to Army

Special OPS

airborne qualification were not only in top-notch physical condition but excelled in the Army's physical training. Before getting the school assignment, the Commanding Officer required Marines to not only maximize the Army's physical fitness requirements but surpass their standards.

The Army required forty-five pushups to pass; ANGLICO needed its Marines to do sixty. The Army had a two-mile run, and passing was 18 minutes; ANGLICO required its Marines to do three miles in 18 minutes. This training allowed excellence in physical conditioning.

Jump School was uneventful. They designated me as the Company Commander of 230 trainees. I spent the next three weeks herding cats and throwing my ass on the ground forty to sixty times a day practicing PLF's (Parachute Landing Falls).

The last event to complete the course was five jumps consisting of four-day jumps and one night jump, all with 60 pounds of combat equipment. After completing the five combat jumps and not breaking any bones, the Army awarded their silver Parachutist Badge (Jump Wings).

I still had to go back to ANGLICO to earn my Marine Gold Wings, which required an additional five combat equipment jumps, three days, and two nights. A month later, I had a second gold device, Jump Wings, to wear above my gold Aviator Wings.

During my 18-month tour in ANGLICO, my job consisted of PT (physical training), airborne operations, classes on controlling bomb-loaded attack aircraft, directing naval gunfire support missions, and supporting the Army mission.

We routinely worked at OP-5, a fifty-foot observation tower on Camp Lejeune that provided visual reference to a bombing range with good visibility of inbound aircraft. But frequently, we went elsewhere to perfect our trade.

A few times a year, a four or five-man team would go to the Naval Training Range, Puerto Rico, on the island of Vieques, six miles east of the mainland. To quote Bill and Ted, "A most excellent place." We used the range to practice our nine-line briefs, a format used for controlling attack aircrafts putting bombs on target. We also practiced naval gunfire techniques whenever a navy ship came to Vieques to qualify in ship gunnery.

The control tower observation post sat atop the range at approximately 600 feet about the impact area. We controlled the bombs on target, but civilians, employed by RCA, managed the range. We hung out in T-shirts and UDT shorts, waiting for the scheduled aircraft to check in. When there were no jets on the schedule, we would have military classes and PT. We always came back from Vieques with a bronze tan, trained on delivering bombs on target, and rested. Shitty job, but someone had to do it.

At least once a year, the whole company, 102 Marines, went to Vieques. We'd do a tactical airborne jump into Camp Garcia, an airfield west of the bombing range. They named the airfield after Marine PFC Fernando Garcia, a Puerto Rican native and Korean War Medal of Honor recipient.

We spent two or three weeks on Vieques doing grunt stuff—map reading, squad tactics, and range fire. On one such deployment, a training event nearly caused a congressional inquiry.

The island's west side was vacant except for wild cattle and horseback Puerto Rican ranchers we called Cowboys. They roamed the unfenced area herding their stock. The terrain in this area was a triple thicket of thorny bushes, baseball-sized spiders, and dangerous swampland.

We used a site free of any civilians to set up one of our M-16 range fire events.

We placed targets against a 10-foot revetment, fifty yards from our firing position. The range safety officer met all the safety requirements. A range OIC (Officer in Charge) was designated. Everything was by the book. For the next two hours, it went as planned. Then, Finagle's Law of Dynamic Negatives entered our training event.

One of the local free-range oxen decided to enter the firing range. The cow's scurried gallop indicated a frightened bovine, either chased by a Cowboy or attacked by one of the many indigenous poisonous snakes.

The reason for the scamper was not apparent, but what was clear, two of the Marines on the firing line decided to empty the rest of their M-16 magazine into the cow. *HOLY CRAP!* They claimed it was an accident.

Irrespective of the claim of accidental discharge and lodging four 5.56 caliber rounds into the brahman, we now had a calamity on our hands. The company first sergeant mused in a calm, controlled voice, "They shot the fucking cow."

Before starting the live-fire exercise, part of the range safety brief highlighted that shooters would immediately cease-fire if any person or thing entered the range. The weapon would be placed on safe and barrels elevated. Sounds straightforward enough, but not to the knuckleheads that continued to fire after Elsey entered their crosshair.

The Safety Officer immediately went to a range safe condition, moved downrange to assess the damage, and radioed back to the rear a "SITREP" (Situation Report). Within an hour (or what seemed minutes), the ANGLICO Commanding Officer was on site with representatives from the island government. Some locals soon arrived and carried off the dead cow, probably to a local meat market for someone's *Carne Quisada* tacos. The Marines were deciding what to do next.

The two Marine assassins' aftermath was a court-martial, heavy fines, and shit canned from ANGLICO back to a grunt unit. The command gave the range OIC an NJP (Article 15, UCMJ) letter of reprimand and a negative performance evaluation. He was also transferred to a grunt unit with his USMC career finished.

As for the martyred heifer? Several Cowboys stepped up, claiming ownership, and received a sizable sum from the US Government. Live fire was not authorized for training on Vieques anymore; the cows were safe.

As if this wasn't crazy enough, another event (we heard from a reliable source—rumor control) happened to our aviator brothers. It seemed a helicopter crew had some extra time on their hands and decided to land on one of the many Vieques empty

The Journey

beaches. After their landing, the four crew members decided to take a swim in the lagoon, stripped down to their skivvies, and plunged into the water.

After a short time, the aviation dolts returned to their aircraft to put on their gear and fly back to base. That's when they discovered a Cowboy had taken their flight suits and boots. With only one option left, they radioed back to their base, explained the problem, and had a jeep drive out to their site with four flight suits and four pairs of boots so they could fly back to base.

An ass-chewing awaited their arrival back at base but was nothing compared to the continuous ball-busting they received for the rest of their now abbreviated Marine Corps career.

Other Marines widely circulated the story amongst their cohorts on the island. Knowing the pilots, this had a degree of believability. As time passed, the story became more aggrandized and embellished. "Did you hear about the Marine helicopter that was stolen?" or, "A couple of Marine pilots drowned while surfing on the beach." As often is the case, the truth lies somewhere in between reality and bullshit.

One of the more insane moments in my tour with ANGLICO happened in October 1983. After arriving home from Beirut, Lebanon, I settled into the company area. I took the time to review my inbox for any important messages and determine what was next in my training or deployment cycle.

A breaking news event hit the TV screen in the company area lounge. The Marines, housed in a parking garage at Beirut International Airport, had suffered a terrorist attack by a truck bomb. No details on how serious it was or the number of fatalities. The Operations Officer called us together and placed us on a "standby to deploy" status. After we checked our gear, we went home to await the call.

Arriving home, I turned on the news to hear the horrifying update of the bombing. In the early Sunday morning of 23 October

1983, a 19-ton yellow Mercedes truck loaded with tons of explosives drove into the four-story parking garage's lower level. It detonated its payload, collapsing the building. The Marines were asleep on various floors in the garage, with the explosion sealing their fate. The blast flattened the structure, crushing the sleeping Marines and killing over 241 military service members.

Shortly after the local news aired the story, I received a call from ANGLICO's Operations to return to base and prepare for deployment. I packed my gear, kissed the wife and kids goodbye (like I have more than a few times), and motored back to the company area. We assumed we were deploying back to Lebanon.

Once inside the company area, a surprise awaited us. We were not deploying back to the Middle East but headed south to a little-known island called Grenada. What the fuck was going on! Nothing was in the news about this isle in the Lesser Antilles archipelago and nothing on our top-secret message traffic. Hell, we didn't even have maps of Grenada.

We scrounged a map of the island from an old National Geographic magazine, printed off two dozen of the reclaimed map of the area, broke up into five teams (one officer and four enlisted per team), and awaited further orders. It didn't take long, and we

The Journey

were on helicopters headed to Fort Bragg, North Carolina, supporting the 82nd Airborne Division.

Once at Bragg, the Army assigned my team to the 1/505th Airborne Battalion. The Army issued us two fragmentation grenades, forty rounds for our M-16, and a training communication book with bogus frequencies.

This communication book and its lack of inter-service operability would later prove problematic. The Army couldn't talk to Navy aircraft, and Navy ships had problems communicating with the Rangers. The Rangers had communication issues with the Marines. Note: this could have been a *cluster fuck* if professional bad guys were in the fight instead of Fidel's Cuban shit bird soldiers.

At Fort Bragg, the atmosphere looked like the real thing, not a peacekeeping boondoggle. Logistics transported the battalion over to Pope Air Force Base, and we boarded C-141 transport planes headed south. We were suited up and ready to jump into Grenada's Point Salines Airport right behind the Rangers. But as we approached the drop zone, the Rangers had secured the airfield, so we stood down.

We took our parachutes off and landed at the airport. The area was secure after the Rangers occupied the high grounds around the airport. Once on the ground, we fanned out in a tactical perimeter. Another grunt battalion was assigned airport security, so we

USMC Grenada

moved out on foot, of course, toward our first objective. We noticed a few dead Cubans soldiers along the road that the Rangers did quick work of.

Our first mission was to secure a campus area at the local university. Intel said approximately 75 US medical students were barricaded, awaiting rescue. Other than Americans' safety, the primary concern was that a hostile government would use them as hostages, as with the 1979 American Embassy takeover in Iran. This motivation put a sense of urgency into our purpose.

We moved quickly to the university site, set up security, and designated an LZ (Landing Zone) capable of landing Blackhawk helicopters.

After a few building searches, we discovered the students hiding in the library. As the door opened, they began to rush out, exhilarated that we found them and confident that they would soon be going home. Student after student came out of hiding, thanking us. The plan now was to put them on inbound Blackhawks and transport them back to Point Salines Airport for further military aircraft flights stateside.

As we moved the students to the LZ, one young man grabbed my shoulder to thank me. We had a few minutes before the next Blackhawk, so I asked him if he would, once stateside, call and deliver a message to my wife. He answered yes. I took out paper and wrote a phone number on it. The note said, "I am south, not east." I asked the student also to tell her you saw me and I was safe and well. I gave the student the note, unsure if the words would get home before I would. When the last student boarded the hello, we cleared the area and went on our next mission.

The Army S-2 had reported the Grenada Military were amassing at Calivigny Barracks, a training compound north of Point Salines Airfield. The Division HQ ordered an air assault by the Rangers. A-7 jets, along with a C-130 gunship, was used as close air support—a bombardment by field artillery was used to prep the assault area.

As the assault began, the lead Blackhawk helicopter, while inserting Rangers near the barracks, approached too fast and crashed landed. The two helicopters behind the lead Blackhawk collided with it, killing three and wounding four. The barracks compound seemed deserted. The American dead and wounded were evacuated.

The next day, our battalion was sent by Division to Calivigny to clean up the mess. When we arrived in the morning, the battalion commander decided to bombard the barracks before going into the area. I called in close air, and A-7's strafed and bombed the area for thirty minutes. After the jets left, an eerie quiet engulfed the target zone.

Then, like a Phoenix rising from the ashes, a large white flag appeared. It looked like some Cubans wanted to surrender? We thought *they must have been some real badasses to survive the assault the night before and to live through the carpet bombing we just called in.*

So, you can understand how dumbstruck we were when a frail, old, brown man came out of a building holding the white surrender flag.

It appeared for months, the old man had been the only occupant of Calivigny Barracks. He was the cantonment caretaker with duties to turn off the lights and keep the wildlife from nesting in the compound.

We reassessed our initial opinion of survivors of the two-day bombardment. They were not badass Cubans, but one tough Grenadian gaffer who, in his younger days, could kick all our asses. We moved on.

The following two days were relatively quiet, except for an ANGLICO team calling in an airstrike on a US Army position, killing one and wounding eleven. This fratricide would carry bad blood between the Army and ANGLICO for some years to come.

I linked up with my Marine pilot buddies at Point Salines Airfield. They told me about fellow squadron mates Seagle, Guigerre, and Sharver getting shot down and killed.

A detailed account of the mission that killed the Cobra pilots, along with the wounding of Captain Tim Howard, is available at the History and Museum Division, Headquarters, U.S. Marine Corps, Washington, DC, search "U.S. Marines in Grenada 1983."

Now that the war was over (5 days fighting, six weeks on the beach), I still needed to get a message to my wife. It just so happened, I came across an M-148 tactical jeep. The jeep was equipped with a sundry of radios, AM, FM, HF (High Frequency).

The HF radio would allow me an attempt to communicate back home. It's been almost a month since I deployed, and indeed my anxious family awaited word from me with the joy of hearing my voice.

As a seasoned aviator trained in radio operations and communication facilities, I quickly figured out how to utilize the M-148 radios and make a linkup. Using the HF, I radioed to MacDill Air Force Base in Tampa, Florida. Once I had a MacDill operator on the line, I requested a linkup with the Camp Lejeune, North Carolina operator. When the Camp Lejeune operator answered, I asked for an official off-base telephone connection.

I gave the Lejeune operator the local telephone number to my wife's office in Jacksonville, North Carolina. Since it was an official off-base call, the operator quickly transitioned from an HF communication frequency to a hardline commercial telephone and patched me into the local official off-base line.

The phone rang three times, and the office secretary answered. I asked for Karen and was told by the secretary, "Please hold." A few minutes passed, and my lovely wife, probably aching from my absence and quivering at the prospect of hearing my voice, answered. Since I was still in a tactical environment, I used a code system I knew she could decipher, hoping her loneliness wouldn't cloud her cognitive ability.

The Journey

I began to speak. "Karen, this is Steve. I am south, not east. I am well and in good health."

The reply was quick, direct, and to the point.

"I know where you are. The medical student you rescued called three weeks ago and said he saw you and you were fine. By the way, where are the damn keys to the truck?" No, *thanks for saving the world for democracy* or *my hero for rescuing all those medical students.* Just a simple "where's the truck keys?"

After telling her where I put the keys to the truck, we bid our adieu before losing our phone linkup. After the call went dead, my reaction was, *what a great lady, letting me play Marine, keeping the home fires warm, and never complaining about my chosen profession.* In ten days, I was home and getting ready for the next deployment.

Grenada

Steve Jacklin

THE CALL

With the pleasured sound of her voice, beauty distance long
Travel is the tenured choice, delightful with first song
Adding joy where there's none makes baleful vista gay
As silence fills with time undone, consider choices weighed

Questions posed "how have you been," answered with a quip
Unstilted, unaffected tone, echoes of a sailing ship
How can you voice and reassure, what's been will always be
A call that's more allure than pure wants and primal needs

Minutes pass to catch up on time, moments that are squandered
Shallow conversations climb, moments will oblige her
Hear me now beyond the waves, a heart that only stumbled
Tomorrow brings to those less brave, enrapture that has crumbled

Speak the words it matters not, just hear your voice again
What is said or long forgot, a dulcet tone has been
Time has passed, the call has dropped, and now with tender broken
I arrive from distance skies, no lovesome verse be spoken

Is there perchance enflamed romance that faded with no plea?
Or has the ship, an endless trip, saw the bottom of the sea
Know not what or where this goes, thoughts of what has been
Vape away like ocean spray, and dial the phone again

Chapter 8
THE OV-10 BRONCO - *"FIRST RULE, MAKE SURE LANDINGS EQUAL TAKEOFFS"*

OV 10 Bronco

In 1985, after six most excellent years as a Huey driver, I opted to transition from helicopters to a fixed-wing OV-10 Bronco. The Bronco was an American-made twin-turboprop light attack and observation aircraft developed in the 1960s as a special operations aircraft for counter-insurgency combat in Southeast Asia. One of its primary missions was a FAC-A (Forward Air Control-Airborne) aircraft.

One of my earliest Vietnam missions was to locate an OV-10 crash site deep in the Que Son Mountains. After finding the Bronco's wreckage, we began shoveling pieces of bodies off the side of the mountain. The pilots were on a counter-insurgency mission in South Vietnam and flew into the side of a rocky peak.

We attempted to identify the body parts, put the remains into body bags, and tag them. Although the dead body's odious smell was overwhelming, we painstakingly continued our recovery efforts. Thoughts of the next of kin experiencing a prolonged pain should we not recover the remains drove our effort. The ethos "leave no one behind" motivated us to complete the extrication.

We called in a helicopter, and two body bags were placed inside the helo for transportation to the morgue in Da Nang, the first stop for the Marine pilots on their journey home.

In the 1980s, the Marine Corps experienced a wave of mishaps within the OV-10 Bronco community, crashing aircraft and killing pilots. The accident review boards would attribute a significant number of these crashes to pilot error. Secretary of the Navy gave the Marines an ultimatum, stop crashing the OV-10, or the Navy will decommission the airframe.

Jacklin with OV-10 1987

The Headquarters Marine Corps' fix was to transfer experienced helicopter pilots into the Bronco cockpits to eliminate pilot errors. This strategy became successful in eliminating the rash of accidents and pilots flying the aircraft into the ground.

I left helos and became a fixed-wing OV-10 pilot. The airframe was exciting to fly with heterogeneity of missions. The Bronco could carry an array of armaments, including four 7.62mm machine guns with 2,000 rounds, external weapons including a gun pod with 20mm M197 electric cannon, and an AIM-9 Sidewinder air-to-air missile. The Bronco was also capable of carrying an array of general-purpose (GP) Mark 80 series bombs, up to and including the Mark 82 (500 lbs.).

The OV-10 was able to load five paratroopers in the back of the aircraft for parachute operations. The rear clamshell door would come off, and five crazy bastards would load and buckle up in the rear of the aircraft.

The OV-10 would take off with the five jumpers, climb to 3000 feet, dive to 200 feet above the ground, and level off with a 250-knot airspeed. Once over the drop zone, the pilot would abruptly nose up 60 degrees. As the Bronco hit 800 feet above the ground, the pilot would flip the green light switch on, the signal to go, the jumpers in the back would see the green light, unbuckle their harness, and as we would say, "shit out the back of the aircraft." A pretty cool mission if you were doing the flying.

In addition to having a great flying experience, I was fortunate to meet some brilliant, professional, somewhat quirky, always entertaining friends.

Case in point, Brian King, with the moniker Budman. He got his call sign by drinking too much Budweiser beer the night before a flight. With a "day after" hangover the next morning, he barfed all over his cockpit. Thus, the Nom De Plume, Budman.

He also had a strange speaking pattern. Budman would start a conversation with an idea construct, complete two sentences, and stop talking mid-sentence. Then he would continue a quiet conversation in his head. His listeners would be waiting for the continuum only to have Budman pick up the conversation two complete sentences later as if he had completed the thought with full, continuous text. We always met his disjointed dialogue with hilarity, amusement, and friendly ballbusting. Budman was one of the good guys.

Another snafu was with Gumston. He checked into the squadron with a self-anointed call sign, Gumby, assuming it would be his given tactical label. That's not how call signs work; the squadron mates needed to vote and approve the moniker. Members voted on his call sign at the next Kangaroo Court, an informal, formal squadron gathering.

A flight school classmate proffered a story about Lieutenant Gumston's suspension from flight training. A hilarious discussion followed, then a vote to change Gumbys call sign, more in line with this flight school event.

It seemed while water skiing in Pensacola Bay, he was struck by the propellers of a ski boat. He was chewed up, spent three months in the hospital, and required an 18-month rehab. A lengthy Navy administrative board review followed, allowing the flight surgeons to medically approve Gumby's further flight training. The watercraft accident scarred most of his body.

The Kangaroo Court heard the mishap's dramatization, the president of the court called a vote, then a new call sign for Gumby was unanimously voted on by the assembled.

On the first ballot, they changed Gumby's call sign to Manatee. This Nom De Guerre would follow Gumston throughout his aviation career. The games continued, and I was back on the road.

The OV-10's aviation radius of travel expanded exponentially from the Huey and our North Carolina base. Due to its increased range over a helicopter, we travel for lunch to Ohio, Mongolian night at the officers' club in NAS Nashville, or lobster runs to Maine.

If we needed a RON (Remain Over Night), we'd take the Bronco to New Orleans, Oklahoma City, or any military base east of the Mississippi River.

Air Force bases would be our primary target for RON's. The accommodations were top-notch, and the officers' clubs had great chow with plenty of cold inexpensive beer.

Other areas we would frequently fly to were CAX and WTI. The CAX was a Combined Arms Exercise the Marines

The Journey

would conduct in the desert of Barstow, California. Marines would train for six weeks in the desert on infantry tactics, tank maneuvers, and artillery firing. Everything was live fire, real bullets, and lots of smoke and sand.

At the end of the six-week training period, a three-day exercise would test what the units had learned. If the evaluations were successful, the Marines would be certified for desert operations.

The WTI (Weapons and Tactics Instructor) school was in Yuma, Arizona. Qualified squadron instructor pilots were sent to Yuma for seven weeks to learn the tactical aspect of flying their machines.

A budget analysis of the training would indicate a cost of over $350,000 per pilot to complete the course. The price was more than an undergraduate degree in a four years Ivy League School.

The OV-10 would participate in the training and support as a FAC (A) for the fixed-wing students. Good flying, great environment.

Capt Jacklin with OV-10

The OV-10D model had FLIR (Forward Looking Infrared) capability. The FLIR cameras used on the Bronco were thermographic cameras that sensed infrared radiation. The sensors installed in the cameras use the detection of infrared radiation, typically emitted from a heat source (thermal radiation), to create an image assembled for video output.

Because of this unique capability and the Bronco's ability to loiter on station over three hours, the squadron picked up a real-world mission from DEA in the early 1980s.

A detachment of four OV-10D's, six pilots, and six backseat observers would deploy to Homestead Air Force Base, located in Southern Florida. Our mission was to fly night operations over Florida's southern coast and identify, using our FLIR, any bogeys (unidentified boats). Once we spotted a bogey, we notified our mission control of the location. If they identified the bogey as suspicious, we would then track the boat until the Coast Guard arrived and intercepted the watercraft.

A famous bootlegger operated out of Southern Florida and the Key West area during the US Prohibition days. The name of the boat used was The Cigarette. It got its name because it was narrower in the beam than the other boats of that era and thus faster. The name would stick.

We spotted a cigarette boat motoring at a fast rate of speed on one such mission, then stopping for as long as three minutes. My observer and I concluded that the boat was stopping, shutting down its engines, and waiting to hear if anyone followed their course.

After the extended shutdown period, the cigarette boat started up and again accelerated to maximum speed. The suspicious boat did this iteration three more times.

Mission control decided we would track the vessel. Since we were operating at night, lights out, above ten thousand feet, and using our FLIR camera for tracking, the bogey didn't know we had a visual track of their activities.

We kept contact with our target for over two hours as the cigarette boat circled off Florida's coast. As the sun began to come up in the East, the bogey made a turn for Miami Harbor, accelerated, and headed straight for the docks.

The Journey

I radioed to mission control the bearing and approximate speed of the cigarette boat. The sun had come up enough to identify the boat's color, and we passed it on to mission control. We followed the cigarette boat for another twenty minutes as it moved into Biscayne Bay.

Off in the distance was a Coast Guard, 33-foot Law Enforcement Special Purpose Craft, hauling ass to intercept the bogey. From the Coast Guard boat's speed and bearing, I could see that it would not catch the bogey before the cigarette boat docked in Dodge Island North. I radioed this information to mission control.

I received a reply to see if I could get the registration number of the boat. Since I was currently at five thousand feet, I would have to descend to a lower altitude. No problem. I nosed the Bronco over and began my accelerated descent toward our target. I briefed my backseater to be ready to take a picture of the boat and note any identifying feature to include any hull marking and registration.

I flew the aircraft, keeping my head outside the cockpit, ensuring we didn't fly into the water at 250 knots. Since they were probably armed smugglers, I told my backseater that we'd do only one pass. After returning to base, we didn't need to explain why there were holes in our fuselage to maintenance control.

At 200 knots airspeed and 150 feet above the water, I began a gradual descent. Approximately a quarter of a mile from the cigarette boat, we level off at 250 knots airspeed and 50 feet above the water. The ocean spray was hitting my aircraft with light steady rain.

Within 200 yards of the bogey, I increased airspeed slightly to ensure that time on target was minimal.

We blew past the target within seconds, enough time to take our pictures, see three hombre armed with automatic weapons, and were quite surprised at our intrusion. I begin a quick climb with a sixty-degree bank angle to the right, away from the boat.

We reported to mission control that we had completed our low pass over the target, identified three armed men, and took pictures of the hull and registration number. The reply from mission control was, "Yazoo One Zero, could you do another low pass to confirm the bogey?"

Since Pablo and his armed cohorts were now alerted to our surveillance, the question of another low fly-by was not an option. After a few cathartic expletives between my backseater and me, I transmitted a one-word radio response to Mission Control, "Negative." They instructed us to continue tracking the boat.

As the cigarette boat approached the Miami piers, they quickly turned from one dock area to another dock, obviously, a diversionary tactic. We continued to track and give position reports to mission control.

The boat finally made a quick stop at one of the loading docks, where a white sedan pulled up, and the three men on the cigarette boat unloaded six large bundles into the trunk of the white car. I passed the information on with an assumption, *"end of the mission, the good guys have won."* Not quite!

The white sedan pulled into an adjacent warehouse. After a few minutes, four identical white sedans exited the warehouse, all in different directions. I shook my head, reported the situation to Mission Control, and returned to base. It looked like the bad guys scored on this one.

Note: my backseater was a career Marine warrant officer named Guy Hunter. After we completed our deployment and returned to North Carolina, I never crossed paths with Guy again. But during the 1991 Iraq war, I turned on my television, and there was Guy Hunter. His OV-10 was shot down over Kuwait, and he was now a POW of the Iraqis. Guy and other Marine aviators would later be released.

The Journey

In 1988, I left Marine Corps active duty and was hired by Eastern Airlines. Unfortunately, shortly after receiving my letter to attend flight training with Eastern, the company laid off 4000 employees and froze all further training and hiring. Due to a major airline strike the next year, Frank Lorenzo, owner of the company, shut the company down and dissolved Eastern.

With that opportunity gone, I went to my backup plan, flying with Piedmont Air. The airline hired me as a commuter pilot with the expectation of moving up to the big boys within six months. Again, my career in the crazy airline industry took another turn.

US Air bought Piedmont Air. This buyout meant a merger of the seniority lists and a swell of additional pilots into the US Air pilot pipeline, all senior to me. Due to seniority, they would be moving up to the regional cockpits before me. US Air said I would have to remain a commuter pilot for at least twenty-four months until the seniority list merged.

US Air expected me to be subsumed for perpetuity into their commuter community. I had other flying options. Since I was dual rated, I decided to go back to helicopter flying. Soon, I was doing some great flying as a Life flight pilot in Cleveland, Ohio.

Steve Jacklin

CHOICES

I've made my choices by listening to voices
Inside a self that resonates, the constant call to congregate
beyond somewhere ... of time and place

I've made my choices, to follow railroad noises
As a beacon call to travel on, the parallel tracks to see what comes
at the end ... but the trips won't end

I've made my choices, beyond all rejoicing
Many routes to far off places, yellow dark, and brown-skinned faces
shape my view ... my world view

I've made my choices, to places that exploited
my moral compass then turned skewed ... playing someone else's tune
as the choir sang the harmony ... off-key

I've made my choices, to love once and only
Forget the time of broken glass, reminisce the loving past
with reverence ... out weighting fitful voices

I've made my choices, the years are enforcing
Thoughts to rise and circumvent, presenting factums I have met
as they disrupt ... my pillowed nights

The Journey

*I've made my choices, don't remind what the price is
I remember my mistakes. I see them all on golden plates
with dreams that echo loud with ache,
of what has happened ... happened yesterday*

OV-10 at Mt. Fuji Japan

HS Graduation 1969

Chapter 9
MY TEENAGE YEARS –
"IN A GADDA DA VIDA"

Flashback, 1965 through 1969, I knew somewhere someone would ask me about my teenage years. Hence, Chapter 9 is an installment of the televised journey of those years.

It was a period disjointed with truth and fabrication, profit and depreciation, pain and merriment.

Like most fourteen to eighteen-year-old boys today, my behavior could have easily been fashionably but incorrectly diagnosed as Attention Deficit Disorder or labeled juvenile delinquency. I would then be given daily doses of Adderall, which the pharmaceutical companies pushed onto the schools through the state and federal government, quid pro quos. I would then be placed in a special education class and sedated through my high school years.

Fortunately, during my sojourn through adolescence, Dr. Spock's books on childrearing were not as popular as they would later become, and the pharmaceutical lobbying efforts in schools were still in their infancy. Thus I avoided any delusive personality diagnosis and a long medication regimen.

In reality, it was just teenage knucklehead stuff, testing boundaries and pushing the outer limits. My goal was to figure out how to grow up, mitigate any screw-ups before reaching maturity, and not do any permanent damage to my future.

One day an aggressive samurai championing his daimyo's honor, the next day, a passive Franciscan monk sitting on a park bench feeding pigeons. One day, a confident youth, the life of the party. The next shindig, a wallflower that couldn't connect two sentences when spoken to by a blonde babe.

Besides being fueled by adolescent hormonal upsurges that amplified the aberrant behavior, I also was beset by a changing culture crucible. No more *Ozzie and Harriet* or *Father Knows Best*. More like *Ray Davies and the Kinks,* with an occasional *Bullwinkle and Rocky*.

I was fielding deep, puzzling, existential questions like, "*Did one of sixteen Vestal Virgins really leave for the coast,*" as Procol Harum's Bach Rock ditty laid out in verse. Why just one Vestal Virgin? Did John Lennon want a *Revolution*, or did John Lennon not want a *Revolution*? And what the fuck was *In-A-Gadda-Da-Vida?* These were some of the perplexing social questions that a struggling generation of teens had to make sense of growing up.

Campus protests and riots were the norms. Racial integration, equality of the sexes, and government transparency were justified causes for demonstration. But most of the campus crisis was simply an opportunity to promote anarchy and disruption to the system. I would later read and discover the unrest was a Bolshevik tactic right out of Saul Alinsky and Norm Chomsky's handbook.

Two Columbia University professors, Cloward and Piven, were also developing strategies for collapsing the capitalist systems by overloading government programs. The revolution was on!

The Weathermen were blowing up military recruiting stations, the Black Panthers were killing cops, and the SDS (Student for Democratic Society) were wrecking college campuses. These sixties nut case radicals intended to tear down the government, take power out of the hands of "The Man," and promote an egalitarian society built on Marxist principles—their tactics similar to the Jacobins in the French Revolution, full of bullshit.

All the sans-culottes needed was a Robespierre and a guillotine to promote *la Terreur.*

Even in my teens, I knew the country had an imperfect union but was working toward the ideas of Hamilton, Madison, Marshall, and the rest of the founding fathers. I was curious about our great Republic's history and always compared it to other global government systems, past and present. I was continually in the critical thinking mode and asking questions about our Republic, like *What was Marbury vs. Madison* or *Why separate drinking fountains for blacks*, and d*id the Monkeys play their own instruments?*

From early on, I felt I had a pretty in-depth understanding of our history and concluded that *America is an idea, not a place.* This aphorism would be the cornerstone of my patriotic fever for the rest of my life. Good people are being guided by the U.S. Constitution, evolving toward the promises of the Declaration of Independence.

As a teen, I would exhibit the usual obnoxious behavior, hiding a panoptic bundle of insecurity. Later I would discover this behavior was not unusual for adolescents. This insecurity, often, was imbued with angst that triggered an obnoxious behavior. "Wish I didn't know now what I didn't know then," Bob Seger 1980. Or put another way, "I didn't make the rules, I just made the rules work for me," Steve Jacklin circa 1970.

Due to my frequent geographic family moves, my scholastic career was dogged with inconsistencies. From grade one through twelve, I attended ten different school systems. I attended three schools in the ninth grade with three different curriculums, teachers, and classmates. When most ninth-graders were building a foundation for further educational growth, it was all I could do to keep up with the correct page in the assigned textbooks.

It seemed that I was always behind in the programmed studies, Geometry, English, Science. It got to the point that the classroom wasn't doing anything for me, my educational journey was stymied, and I was bored shitless. So, I said screw it, skipped school, hung out on the beach surfing, and began self-tutoring. The only reason I attended class was football or basketball season. I played and started both sports. "When I look back on all the crap I learned in high school, it's a wonder I can think at all," Paul Simons, 1973

One of the three schools I attended in my ninth grade was at Wheelus Air Force Base in Libya. The family moved to Tripoli during the last two months of my freshman year in high school. I had made several friends four months earlier in Toledo, Ohio (second school of my high school freshman year), and now was forced to leave them. While bouncing around to different schools, different social groups, and various tribes, you learned to either be quick with your wit or with your fists, always needing to prove yourself.

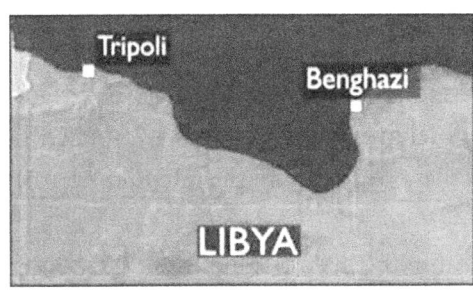
Libya 1967

I did have a significant advantage, though. I was a good (often) great athlete. I loved basketball, played point guard, and averaged 15 points a game. I also played football and was told I still hold receiving records at my high school in Ohio. Wow, a slow white boy, forty-nine years later, still on the record books. It sure doesn't say much for my high school's passing game the last four decades.

My days in Libya were, at times, rough and confusing. I am a fourteen-year-old pubescent boy, leaving a great group of friends in Ohio, traveling across the world, and now living with four

The Journey

younger siblings in an orange grove, isolated from my peer group. My life was anchored twenty miles from anyone my age, with an orchard homestead environment that seemed whacked out.

So, what did I do, make lemonade out of lemons? Na, the saying I found threadbare, trite, and a lazy axiom. Instead, I lived by my original adage; *solitude hones potentiality*. More authentic than a silly outro about the virtues of making citrus juices from lemons. What I did was spend the summer teaching myself to play the guitar and piano. I also practiced dribbling the basketball a few hours a day. I became a good ball handler and musician.

My days in Libya were something out of a Franz Kafka novel. Not a metamorphosis of a fourteen-year-old boy turning sixteen. More like *The Castle,* with ossified missteps and alienation, often requesting permission to live in the village. The years, post-fifteenth birthday, followed me with plenty of dysfunctionality and excitement.

Because we lived off the Air Force base, I had full rein to hang out or do all kinds of dumb-ass stuff with my cohorts. Case in point; I played guitar, so I'd ride the bus on Friday and bring my axe (guitar) to school. Someone would have a gig that night, so I'd stay after school and get with the rest of the band. Remember, I lived isolated on a Libyan orange grove, 20 miles off base, in BFE (Bum Fucked Egypt).

1969

We'd play the gig, usually two hours, get our ten bucks apiece and decide where to crash. If on base, we'd stay at one of the band members' houses. I'd prefer Jeff, our drummer, because he had an older sister who was hot, at least in the eyes of a fifteen-year-old gawker. Since we had no phone system available, there was no way to contact my mom and let her know my plans (fake or otherwise) for the weekend.

We experienced problems if we played in a Tripoli nightclub or cross-town at the American oil compound. We needed to find a place to crash and find transportation to haul our drums.

We would carry our guitars and a few times crashed on the beach. This sleeping arrangement presented its own set of problems with the locals. Some of the Berber tribes of Libya were remarkably tolerant of gay behavior. The Libyan adult males prefer white boys over burka-covered Libyan females. It was common knowledge to the American teens that sodomy was practiced amongst the local tribesmen and was culturally acceptable, despite Islam's condemnation against homosexuality. Getting snatched would cause some long-term damage to your libido.

Tripoli

The other option was the go-to preferred option, crash on someone's roof. The residential houses had an architectural design with a flat roof and a ladder on the house's side to access the top. We randomly picked a place, scurried up the ladder to the roof, and slept the night away. We never had an issue with our housetop nightly slumbers.

The next day we hitched rides back to the club and picked up our drums. If all things worked out, we'd have a second gig that weekend. Then after "jamming" Friday and Saturday night, we found something to do on Sunday.

Monday morning, we went to school and took the bus home Monday afternoon. Sounds like the perfect schema, huh? Not quite. Being a fifteen-year-old teenager in a foreign country and a mother having no idea where her son was for four days did prove problematic.

Leaving Friday morning and not showing up again till Monday afternoon was another dumb-ass trick. I wasn't doing anything wrong in my teenage mind, not stealing cars, smoking dope, or having sex with young Catholic girls (the beatas would come later). I could not figure out why mom was so upset. I saw myself as the perfect idyllic son.

Later in life, as a father of three daughters, I would come to appreciate the gravity of these stunts and would embody a special sympathy and love for my mother's act of courage in raising me.

Note, my mom has a special place in heaven for trying to raise me during those teenage years. As for me, because of my many shenanigans, I'm still trying to "good deed" myself out of purgatory.

I decided not to put my mother through these traumatic events anymore. Did I quit playing in the band and stop going AWOL over the weekend? Hell no! Whenever we had a gig, I would just tell her Friday morning I would be staying at Dave's house over the weekend and back Monday after school. She didn't need to know what roof I was sleeping on and give herself unnecessary grief. On one occasion, she did ask why my clothes had sand in them and if Dave lived next to the beach. We never had a Dave in the band.

Another time, we decided to party on the beach, fifteen miles from downtown Tripoli. Jenson was a senior, had a car, and had a Libyan driver's license. He piled five of us into his Renault and dove us to the impromptu beach party.

In the trunk of the car were four cases of Miller Lite beer. We found a dirt road just off the highway, followed it down to the beach, and unloaded the beer and guitars. We gathered some firewood and settled into a quiet, comfortable party venue, something right out of a 1950's *Gidget* beach movie.

It wasn't more than an hour, and we had company. A pair of headlights were coming down the dirt road. We put the fire out, and Jenson crawled, then ran to his Renault.

The oncoming vehicle's movement was slow, with occupants shinning spotlights on each side of the trail. We keep motionless for a few moments waiting to see who our party crashers were. As the vehicle got closer, we could see it wasn't a police car.

The small truck stopped about fifteen yards from us, and three Arab men, with clubs, exited the vehicle. The interlopers' tones were aggressive and loud, probably hopped up on hashish. We all concluded they were after our beer and our virginity, more the latter than the brew.

The five of us were separated and spread out over the dunes, cactus, and beach vegetation—everyone for themselves, camouflaged in their denizen, with a prearranged escape plan. We agreed to rendezvous back on the highway, where Jenson would pick us up.

The interlopers moved quickly through the area, swirling their flashlight beams randomly and beating the brush with their clubs. One tramper came as close to me as ten feet. I laid quiet as his flashlight scanned the area he hoped to plunder.

A few moments passed, and the gadfly moved away from my borehole, allowing me to start moving slowly toward the dirt road. Once a sufficient distance from detection, I broke out into a full sprint. After reaching the dirt road, I tracked it to the highway. Once I got to the main drag, I again found concealment and waited for Jenson's Renault to extricate me from this shit storm.

I bided my time, hidden for about thirty minutes when I saw headlights coming down the highway. Every minute, the headlights would come on and off three times. The flashing was our prearranged signal for pickup. As the vehicle came nearer to my position, I moved into the highway centerline and began unflaggingly waving my hands over my head like a survivor from the Lusitania.

The car came to a stop. I identified the Renault driver and climbed into the back seat. I was the last one to be picked up.

Since all the sand dune, puerile dorks were accounted for, Jenson got the hell out of the area. We lost the beer but saved our virginity—just quintessential American teenagers hanging out on a beach in Libya.

Other moments stick into my head and produce a smile and sometimes outright laughter. I was riding in a car with Italian friends cruising downtown Tripoli. My Italian was weak, but thankfully, their English was good. They had the Rolling Stones playing on their car speakers. After the third playing of the song, *Satisfaction*, I questioned how the song was repeating since the radio was off.

Downtown Tripoli

Remember, this was 1966, the days before eight tracks, cassette, and no streaming music loops. They gave me that "look what we did" shit-eating grin and preceded to open the car's glove compartment.

They had configured a sound system mounted within the glove compartment that would play a 45 RPM record. The compartment was configured with a floating base that would absorb bumps and a small turntable with the record *Satisfaction*. It had an adjustable arm with a mounted play needle attached to the arm. The needled arm would lower and access the grooves on the record. Once the needle made contact with the record grooves, the song would play through the front and back twelve-inch German-made stereo speakers with the bass woofer pounding 4/4 time on the floor.

The music rocked, the volume was excessive, and the car vibrated. The locals appeared to find displeasure in our decadent behavior. Wow! Totally crazy!

I lost touch with Tony and Marcello, my Etruscan pals, but assumed they were making lots of money somewhere with an internet startup company.

Another life moment was a basketball tournament in Italy. The Base high school team didn't have other American high school teams to play, so our regular scheduled league consisted of playing Air Force service members on base. We had a second league playing in town against Italian high school players. The cool thing about playing in town was we used the international basketball rules.

Every year the Department of Defense would sponsor a tournament for high school teams in the Mediterranean area. The games would be in Northern Italy at an Army base in Vicenza. Along with cheerleaders, the team would leave Libya, fly to Rome, spend two days, and then fly to the tournament.

Since we had three senior starters who played in the games the year before, our team was the favorite to win the tournament again. Larry Harris was one of the returning seniors and a hell of a power forward who averaged eighteen points a game in the previous year's tournament. He also pulled down forty rebounds in three games.

He had major college potential but had his athletic career goals set on becoming a professional bowler. No shit!

I don't recall seeing a black, 6 foot 4 inch, professional bowler on the PBA Tour, so I assumed Larry took one of the many basketball scholarships offered him and pursued a career as a lawyer or hedge fund manager. I'm also sure he was the MVP of his Tuesday night bowling league.

The whole trip was *a trip*. Were it not for the stopover in Rome, the tournament championship would have been ours. But

The Journey

the problem was the stopover in Rome. This hiatus is where the other fifteen-year-old scholar-athletes and I discovered cheap Italian wine and American cheerleaders.

By the time we hit Vicenza, the team was in no condition to play basketball. We got bounced in the first round, played in the consolation bracket, and lost again. It took me a week to recover from the debacle. Rome wasn't built in a day, nor can fifteen-year-olds drink all the Italian wine in a day and play basketball.

Life lesson! From that point on in my many adult travels, I would always get the work and sightseeing done first, then imbibe myself with fine local spirits.

Another significant event in my Libyan travels was my early departure from the Middle East. The morning of June 5th, 1967, was one of the craziest events, not only in my youth but in my life.

I had missed the school bus and would catch a ride to the base school with my mom. My younger sister was also home due to her kindergarten teacher having an end-of-the-school-year workshop. The early morning was usually quiet on the orange grove homestead, but not today.

A loud uproar was happening outside on the road to the entrance of our villa. The Arab workers, ordinarily docile, were engaged in angry chatter. Since neither mom nor I could speak enough Arabic to understand what was happening, we turned on the local radio.

As we scrolled through the local Arab stations, we could hear something big was going on. We finally were able to tune into the English-speaking Armed Forces Radio Station and hear the news. Crap! Shit had hit the fan!

After the Arab League massed troops along three fronts for an eventual invasion of Israel, the IDF (Israeli Defense Force) initiated a defensive preemptive assault.

The IDF had launched an attack on the Egyptians in the Sinai. They used jets to bomb the Syrians on the Golan Heights and used infantry and tanks on Jordanians in the West Bank. Because the IDF secured all its primary military objectives and solidified its borders in six days, this became known as the Six-Day War.

So much for the tactics and geopolitics of our domicile, now what did we do next? We did what we had to.

We quickly loaded up the car with all the personal items we could carry, knowing locals would loot and "ratfuck" the house once we left. I pulled out the two loaded guns we had, a shotgun and a pistol, and then strapped into the front passenger seat of the family sedan. My younger sister laid flat on the floor in the back of the green '59 Buick. I put the pistol in the glove compartment and held the readied shotgun on my lap.

We slowly approached the entrance to the local highway when a crowd of Arabs moved to block our exit. Mom floored the gas pedal and accelerated. The rapid acceleration caused the car to backfire—the crowd dove for cover from the perceived gunfire. Mom drove aggressively through the dispersed locals and exited, what would be, no longer our home.

Our twenty-mile trip back to the Air Base was like a roller derby championship match. Once we were on the local road that took us to the base, angry mobs would intercept the family sedan and try and stop our car.

Mom would swerve, attempt to avoid hitting anyone. The rioters would dive clear of her speeding pugnacity. Nothing would stop this wolverine mother from getting her cubs to safety.

On one stretch of the road, the mob built a barrier across the street with burning tires and a donkey cart. Our vehicle veered to the left of the barricades, ran over some debris, settled back onto the road, and continued our Great Escape.

The Journey

As Mom accelerated, the pissed-off manic crowd would give way to her oncoming Buick. It looked like a scene from the movie *The Ten Commandments* with Moses parting the Red Sea.

It took us over an hour to navigate twenty miles and arrive safely onto the airbase with four flat tires. From the look of the car, Mom didn't hit or run over anyone, and I still had all the bullets I started within the chamber of my gun. We were safe on Wheelus Air Force base with no harm, no foul.

We picked up my other two brothers and sister at their school and began preparing for the evacuation process from what was now a hostile country. End of story? Nope.

Two days later, we were on a military transport aircraft, with other vomiting military dependents, headed to Torrejon Air Force Base near Madrid, Spain. Once we landed, we were moved to the American side of the airfield and housed in the enlisted airmen's quarters. The accommodations were adequate, with expectations of being there overnight. The U.S. State Department was arraigning commercial transportation back to the states.

The overnight turned into five days with the families confined to the housing area—nothing to occupy five kids except kicking a soccer ball and grab-assing.

Every morning at eight o'clock, a bus transported the families to base flight operation and herded us into a hangar area to hear our names called for transportation home. This process lasted an hour or two. If the officer in charge did not call your family's name, you would be bused back to the housing area to continue your soccer ball grab-assing and wait for the next day's roll call.

After the third dull day, I was becoming bat shit crazy. Having just experienced an insane adrenalin rush evacuating Libya, the seventy-two hours of nothingness presented problems for this fifteen-year-old man-child. On the fourth day, I opted to liven things up, at least for me.

I had never been to a bullfight, not a lot of matadors in Libya. Since they didn't call our names for a return flight home at the morning roll call, I decided to experience my first bullfight extravaganza.

I heard from an airman on the base that the fights were a daily afternoon event in downtown Madrid. So, I hitched a ride into town, walked five blocks, and found the arena. I had just enough money for admission and slid into a fifth-row seat.

Pretty cool, the whole pageantry, spectacle, and ritual inside the *Plaza de* Toros was a lavish Spanish cultural presentation. I wasn't entirely sure what was going on or why the crowd cheered when they did, but the applause's excitement caused me to throw my hands together with enthusiasm. It was like watching a hockey game, not knowing any of the rules, just waiting for the fight to break out. A couple of hours passed watching this spectacle.

The *banderillero* worked with his decorated sticks stabbing the bull's neck, pissing the bull off while the matador put on a show. He seemingly sentenced the bull to death, and then, with the *estocada*, he administered the death blow with his sword.

Sorry about that Mr. Bull. I Sincerely hoped his death had some sacrosanct meaning, like ending up on a beef taco.

I would learn the bullfight dance had an old tradition that harkens back to ancient times with man's deep fear of death and his ability to overcome it. The matador won, the bull lost, and the crowd when nuts.

After the last *corrida* (bullfight), I made my way through the crowd and hitched a ride back to the base. I was gone slightly over four hours. Upon arriving at the base housing area, I checked in with Mom to find her outraged and ready to perform an *estocada,* on me. Luckily, she didn't have a sword in hand.

It seemed base flight operations did an additional roll call in the afternoon, adding names of passengers to leave in two hours on the next plane. They called the Jacklin family, but Mom told the colonel in charge that she could not take the flight due to my absence and not knowing my whereabouts. It looks like the bull won this one. The Jacklin family left on the next plane in the morning, and my price to get out of purgatory just kept adding up.

It seemed every moment I spent in Libya had its elevated level of chaos and exhilaration. One would think I had enough excitement in those three years to last a lifetime, but no. It only produced a chronic habitual compulsion for that adrenalin rush. For the rest of my life, I would be pushed toward the outer limits of societal parameters, always seeking that euphoric recall. I could have easily become a hobo riding the railway.

Fortunately, my positive moral compass controlled my compulsive personality and channeled the energy into a more favorable outcome. Still, I was always looking down those railroad tracks, wondering where they would take me.

After returning from Libya, I spent the next two years finishing high school in Groveport, Ohio. I had a modicum level of athletic success, enough to catch the eye of a few college coaches vying for my ability to catch a football. But I opted for another journey down the railroad tracks, and I joined the Marines.

Steve Jacklin

BEYOND

Time between the morning and the dreams
Lays thoughts of never-ending moments
Yesterday speaks to beyond what is able to hold tight
Lifts the solace dreams and move into the blast zone

Close the moments and welcome the passing
Have you paid enough to the driver of the vehicle
Have you given enough of yourself, leaving not anything on the field
Is there still enough bright to continue beyond

Press and compressed the taproot to level the resistance
Failure to allow even the slightest degree of thought dispersion
If the ability to share has been extinguished
Then the ability to ensure species survival is for not

Underlining all the froth presents a dessert unlike chocolate mousse
The tasteful delight is unwelcomed in genteel circles
The epic tiramisu is not acceptable to the palette of the Francophiles
Xenophobia now sets the oven temperature, the sign reads
"English Speakers Only"

It's now time to share a sleep, travel to a nocturnal woolgather
Knowing that the time is steep, a climb not always gallant
Once awakened by the aurora and obnoxious feathered bastards
Is there still enough bright to continue beyond

Chapter 10
ENTER MY FOURTH DECADE - *"AS I COUNT THE RINGS ON THE TREE"*

I spent the 1990's flying helicopter air ambulance, some of the best flying I experienced in my aviation career. Flying "Life Flight," the colloquial term for air ambulance missions, is similar to a fireman. You have a base where you would wait for dispatch to call. Once you get the call, you have five minutes to check the weather to ensure you can get there and back safely, then take off. When you arrive at the scene, you get a landing zone brief from the on-scene commander and check the landing zone clear of obstacles. After landing, the medical crew disembarks from the aircraft and evaluates the medical situation. Once triaged and packaged, the patient is loaded into the helicopter and transported to a hospital. Sounds easy, huh?

Grant Lifeflight

The flying was exciting and rewarding, although the type of medical transport was not without its issues of tragedy and foreboding. The actual trauma scene's shivery would be magnified by dread, knowing the horror the family would soon experience. Next of kin would occasionally be on the accident scene or meet the helicopter crew upon landing at the hospital. The emotional encounters were tormenting and haunting.

The PTSD factor was a significant issue in the daily life of a trauma flight crew. Image, a flight to a scene of an accident. Upon arriving at the crash, you find a family of four hit by a drunk driver, all dead, except the drunk driver. Mom didn't wear a seatbelt, was ejected out the passenger door, now lying in a ditch with her thirty-something body broken. The two children in the back seat, still buckled into their car seats, mangled beyond identification. The father, who was the driver, decapitated. Inside the van's interior, the crash's impact painted a macabre fresco of magenta hurt. The drunk driver was not injured and was flown to the hospital for evaluation.

Or a seven-teen-year-old motorcyclist, without a helmet, running into a tree, leaving his skull split opened from back to front. His female rider had both legs torn from her torso, bleeding profusely. Neither one would make it to the hospital alive.

Worst yet, while babysitting, grandma turns her back for a second, and now paramedics are pulling her two-year-old grandson from a backyard swimming pool. Watching the doctor break the news to the parents at the hospital that the young boy died was difficult. The parents' sadness was overwhelming. The grandmother will carry the guilt to her necropolis.

These daily tragic engagements would leave marks on all involved as if an artist uses a thick impasto technique to complete a morbid masterpiece within the soul. The crew will experience a heavy heart yet, the next day, do it again.

The Journey

Case in point, on a summer day in 1994, our crew was dispatched to a potential drowning in Southern Ohio. The scene was a dirt road next to a farmhouse with a dusty road leading to a pond at the bottom of a hill.

When we arrived, the local fire department pulled a car from the pond, with two young boys still buckled in their car seats. The vehicle had been submerged for over an hour. Since there were two infant patients, the fire department called for a second helicopter for transport.

Medflight over Columbus skyline

Upon extracting the infants from their car seats, the medical crew immediately did a triage. Bodies were cold, with no pulse or breathing detected on either of the boys. We airlifted the bodies to the hospital for an attempted resuscitation. The rule for drowning victims was, "Not dead until warm and dead."

We immediately flew to the closest hospital and moved the young boy into the emergency room. The mother met us at the hospital, and the husband soon joined her. The police immediately begin questioning the hysterical mother about what happened; this is where tragedy would be highlighted by ill-disposed behavior.

The mother told the police she parked on the hill, left her boys in their car seats, ensured she engaged the emergency brake, and shut the ignition off. She then climbed over a fence, went across a field to feed the cows. She said the emergency brake must have disengaged and rolled down the hill with her boys still buckled in their car seats. Not sure if there were criminal findings with any investigation.

Another grim happening was a flight we made in the winter of 1996 to Southeast Ohio. A young couple was building a house on a lake. The construction was almost complete, and the mom and dad were doing a final walkthrough. While the couple was in the new home with the contractor, their two young sons, 8 and 10, decided to play on the ice-covered lake. Unfortunately, the freeze didn't hold the two youngsters, and the lads fell through the ice. As we arrived on the scene, the fire department was attempting to find the drowned boys. We waited approximately three hours and then returned to base without transport. The fired department recovered the two bodies the next day.

All the flying wasn't entirely dark; some had comical overtones. One such flight we called the "Stanley Cup Escapade." In 1997, Columbus, Ohio, was given a National Hockey League (NHL) franchise. The team was named The Columbus Blue Jackets with Nationwide Insurance, a major sponsor.

Off-loading Staley Cup from Medical Helicopter

The Nationwide Insurance marketing team came up with an idea to promote the upcoming team's inaugural foray into a football town. They had the NHL approve the transportation of the Stanley Cup to Columbus. Once in town, a helicopter would fly in, land, and load the Cup on a stretcher. The aircraft would fly to predetermined public relations venues with the Stanley Cup strapped onto the stretcher. The helicopter would land, unload the Stanley Cup, and do the marketing presentation. The marketing committee chose Midflight of Ohio to supply the transport vehicle.

As if a four-foot hockey trophy, strapped to a medical gurney, exiting a medical helicopter wasn't crazy enough, the NHL "head shed" decided to add an extra layer of security. After the helicopter shutdown, the side door would slide open. Out stepped a sentry, over six feet tall, clad in a dark blue suit, black tie, white shirt, and white gloves. His demeanor was stoic, impassive, and humorless. His unruffled, emotionless persona could have easily been confused for a member of the Queen's Guard on duty at Buckingham Palace.

After shutdown, and at my direction, the guard relocated, using marching steps, to the back of the aircraft. The door opened, and there was the focus of his guardianship, the Stanley Cup.

Stanley Cup with Security Guard

The NHL sent the security agent to ensure nothing happened to the Cup. Since the Cup did have a storied history of misadventures, I assumed the escort was to prevent another debacle with the silver goblet. From urinating in the Cup to throwing the trophy into the river, stories were widely circulated about the travels of this iconic vessel. I guess kidnapping the Stanley Cup was a real possibility.

We pulled the gurney from the back of the helo and began rolling it to the marketing event. The stoic guard marched next to the Cup with a vigilance seen only by secret service agents protecting the President. One crewmember attempted to help the white-gloved sentry but was rebuffed by the watchman since the crewmember wasn't wearing white gloves. No one would touch the trophy!

The Cup, bound tightly to the wheeled stretcher, was steadfastly guarded by the humorless devoted sentinel. His presence remained rugged and unflappable. Children surrounded the gurney, along with adult hockey fans. Visible were local politicians who needed to capitalize on the moment and get a picture for the local news with the Stanley Cup, as if they invented the game and personally secured the franchise for Columbus.

These marketing events continued for six more landings. Same drill; land, shutdown, unload, march the Cup to an awaiting crowd; smile, pictures, and then leave. After a while, boredom and my propensity for impropriety overtook me, so I decided to break up the monotony.

I approached the gaggle and stood abeam the sentry. I launched a gibe toward the Cup's Canadian protector with a raised tone and volume level loud enough for the crowd to hear. "Mr. Chiclets, I understand basketball is the favorite sport for most children in your country. But around ten years old, they realize they can't jump, nor do they have a left-hand dribble. All they have are ponds that freeze solid nine months a year and the ability to take a left hook to the chin, so they decide to play hockey. With a limited supply of black athletes in Canada, you're then forced to make hockey your national sport. Unfortunately, a sport you now become a close second behind the Russians."

I made my taunt in jest to lighten up the afternoon, not for an acrimonious ball-busting. The crowd snickered, chuckled, and smiled with a barely auditory "oh shit" gasp. Our Stanley Cup

Templar broke modus and appeared to have a vague smile on his lips. But his eyes gave me a menacing glance that advised me it was time to get back into the helicopter before he was "boarding" me against the "half wall." All was good.

Air ambulance flying was my full-time job, but I also was an Ohio Army National Guard member. Guardsmen frequently told the active Army, "Your job is my hobby," and referred to the financial remuneration in the guard as "Yuppie Welfare." Of course, this was all pre-9/11. The atmosphere was casual; the training was insouciant, with only superficial efforts toward military ethos.

Illustrating this point was my first summer Army training iteration, two weeks in Grayling, Michigan. The National Guard training was to provide a pleasant nonacrimonious setting, not designed to produce part-time warriors. The goal was to allow a guardsman an idyllic experience, thus wanting to stay in the guard, reenlist and do it again next year.

The pre-9/11 National Guard's emphasis was unit strength, not for preparation for any military conflict but to ensure the units would not be downsized by headquarters or, worse, disbanded due to low manning levels. If the unit dropped below required personnel strength numbers, they could be on the deactivation list. If a state lost a battalion or brigade, it meant money and promotional opportunities sent to another state that met its personnel quota, thus denying the opportunist the fortune to continue their fortune.

I didn't know and won't understand how this fallacious mandate would manifest itself for a few years, but I immediately sensed a disconnect at my first annual training departure formation.

Since the organization had been making this summer training trip for the last fifteen years, same place, same dates, same people, the brigade didn't furnish a packing list for deployment. A few weeks earlier, I asked a couple of old-timers what I should bring and how to pack in preparation for the training. They gave a nonchalant shrug and a matter-of-fact, "Bring what you normally bring to the field." OK, sounded simple; I'd done this field training exercise many times before.

As the scheduled due date for the field training moved forward, I broke out my field pack. I made a list of what I would need to survive two weeks in Michigan's wild backcountry. I checked off four pairs of socks, three t-shirts (Army brown), five pairs of underwear, an extra set of camouflage utilities, sunscreen, insect repellant, toiletries, poncho, zip lock bags for waterproofing, rain gear, and a few other odds and ends.

The day before our departure into the bush, I carefully loaded my pack and properly distributed the weight. The straps were adjusted for weight dispersion, allowing comfort with any length of combat march we may have to make.

The following day, I arrived at the unit staging area, dressed in my best battle gear; helmet, green Army camouflaged utilities, a canteen strapped to my left hip, and a medical pouch attached to the other hip. The only thing missing was my face painted up with camouflage. So, you can guess my incredulity when this "high speed, low drag, killing machine" arrived and saw how my cohorts had prepared to do battle.

My first reaction was a "holy shit" moment. On display as battle dress and military continuity were an array of shorts and tennis shoes, "catch me, fuck me" t-shirts with a sundry of messages printed on the front or back. Most were funny (In My Defense I Was Left Unsupervised), some political (Ted Kennedy's Car Killed More People Than My Gun), and a few misogynistic (Don't Be a Sexist Bitches Hate it) messages.

In addition to the fashion cornucopia, the eclectic battlefield equipment readied for deployment was festive and functional, that is, if en route for a two-week family vacation to the Magic Kingdom. The cadre had jet skis attached to Ford 150

The Journey

pickup trucks, boats with trailers pulled behind four-wheel-drive vehicles, ATV's and QUADs transported via Dodge RAM's, canoes, and kayaks mounted atop SUVs.

The packing list consisted of various one-person tents, golf clubs, tennis rackets, Weber portable grills, TVs, civilian clothes (lots of civilian clothes), and an occasional uniform. I stood there in momentary bemusement, realizing this was to be a *mucho* merriment experience.

The looks I received were ubiquitous, with an occasional "Fucking Jarhead" comment. I blew off the sentiments and ignored the looks while adjusting my attitude to a less aggressive, more National Guard in vogue conviviality. I took off my helmet, unbuckled my ammo belt, and loaded my gear on the truck. I found my assigned ride to the Michigan training area and settled into an eight-hour tortuous journey in the backseat of a HUMVEE. Two weeks later, the blithe gathering was over with another eight-hour tortuous HUMVEE return trip home. Thus, I began my fifteen-year Army National Guard career.

Later on, during one of the summer two-week training events, I was the commanding officer, responsible for moving the battalion six hundred miles from three locations to train in Grayling, Michigan. We moved over 350 soldiers, 75 vehicles, and 18 helicopters up and back safely without losing any aircraft, vehicles, or soldiers injured. By all accounts, the fifteen days was a resounding success. My guidance to the staff and officers was working hard, training hard, and keeping the bullshit down to a minimum.

The "Hoe Throw" tournament games became a training highlight of this deployment. I've always subscribed to the theory of MWA, (Management by Walking Around). The Command Sergeant Major and I would do an evening walk around the airfield tent area and an early morning run around the same place. The purpose of the evening walkabouts was to ensure everyone was settled down and quiet for the night. We observed a humorous, gut-splitting event on one of our early MWA's, albeit not necessarily a politically correct occurrence.

The setting—a kiddie's 3-foot blue plastic swimming pool, thirteen Army warrant officer pilots drinking Coors Beer sitting around the pool in lawn chairs, and a 24-inch rubber donut floating inside the plastic kiddie pool.

A rubber swimsuited blonde Barbie doll, found in any young girl's toy box, was being prepped for launch into the donut hole. There appeared to be a scorekeeper with a notepad in the back of the seated aviators. As the Sergeant Major and I got closer to the tent area, we heard a commotion, immediately followed by a kerfuffle each time someone appeared to register a score.

The pilots would get a turn to throw the bikinied Barbie into the rubber donut. Four teams were competing against each other to see who could score in the collegial contest. A team member would toss Barbie into the pool and aim at the donut. Each time Barbie submerged into the donut hole, it registered a score. The participants hollered a string of acclamations and boos at each score, followed by a few expletive ululations. The Hoe Throw games were a team-building exercise, generating high morale, and beer-drinking to a minimum. No harm, no foul.

I called the senior warrant officer over to discuss the event. I told him to ensure the area was cleaned up and looked like a military billeting area when I made my walk around in the morning.

At first dawn, the Sergeant Major and I did our MWA. There it was, the area cleaned, pristine, and ready for inspection. The swimming pool was hidden from view, the beer cans thrown in the recycled bin, lawn chairs folded and stashed inside the tents with Barbie on vacation.

But the pilots had to have the last word. They constructed a two-foot official-looking military camouflaged sign posted at the tent area entrance, with a white-lettered acronym NAMBLA, not the trademarked North American Man/Boy Love Association but Navy, Army, Marine, Buoyancy Laboratory Area. I duly noted the satire with an under my breath chuckle and a nod to the Sergeant Major. I let the sign stay up until the First Army arrived to inspect the battalion the following week.

"My Bad" ... the Oxford Dictionary defines the phrase as a mea culpa or *my fault* or *my mistake*. Another interpretation of this colloquialism would be, "I fucked up, sorry about that." This phrase delineation was illustrated by a day VFR training flight I took with a new second lieutenant right out of flight school.

I practiced maneuvers that took the aircraft low to the ground with airspeed and bank angle at the envelope's outer limits: no aerial acrobatics, just aggressive helicopter flying. After a few iterations, I turned the controls over to the left seat copilot. Her first attempt at the maneuver was slow and deliberate. I thought, pretty safe. But as she progressed, her confidence level exceeded her experience and talent. Abruptly she put the aircraft into a bank angle and nose-down attitude that exceeded the maneuvers' safety norms.

As the airspeed increased and the ground got closer, I took physical control of the helicopter, leveled the aircraft, and climbed to a safe altitude.

Once perched at fifteen hundred feet above the ground and level, I gave a "what the fuck" look to my copilot, to which I received the contrition, "My bad." My annoyed retort would be, "Excuse me, Lieutenant." My expectation with the "excuse me, Lieutenant" exclamation was to receive a thoughtful explanation as to what just happened, not a casual "My bad." But something was lost in our exchange; what I received back was, "My bad, **sir**."

We terminated the training flight and returned to base. We debriefed the flight, talked about the botched maneuver. I concluded the debrief by giving the young Lieutenant a professional lesson on military courtesy and suggested removing MY BAD from her aviation lexicon. The Lieutenant went on to have a very successful aviation career.

The combat readiness of the National Guard during the 1990s was problematic at best. As long as the "Weekend Warriors" weren't needed to engage in hostilities, the charade was undiscoverable.

The Bill Clinton Administration pulled a sham over the American people. The Administration cut the military budget, primarily in the combat support and combat service support units in the Reserve and National Guard. By doctrine, these units were to support the active Army with immerging conflicts.

During Bubba's presidency, a shortage of personnel, no training dollars, degraded equipment readiness, and maintenance issues characterized the Reserve and National Guard military.

The unit readiness report numbers were massaged to show a higher level of preparedness for war. This technique would ensure the senior officers could continue in their upward promotional trajectory. The senior civilian staff didn't dig deep into the readiness numbers either, lest they bring to light the "hollow force." We saw the duplicity and shortcomings of this strategy when we mobilized and tried to send the hollow force to war post 9/11. We weren't ready but got ready real quick.

I came into the National Guard as a warrant officer and left the Guard fifteen years later as a Lieutenant Colonel. I say that only to bring up the fact after my initial misdo, I successfully learned to navigate the political apparatus and cultural system of my part-time vocation. As I've said before, "I don't make the rules; just made the rules work for me."

Fifteen years later, I was active duty Army with a country at war.

The Journey

BABY BOOMERS

As I count the rings on the trees
It suddenly dawns on me
I remember all I see
Looking at a young one turning three

Things I liked back in 64'
I don't find it entertaining anymore
Jagger and the Stones are now a bore
With his wrinkled harmony
Singing to his guitar lead

I like the music they still play
The bass guitar and drummer sound the same
But when I see them on a TV show
They look like old men playing rock and roll
Turn the reverb up to hind the notes they can't make
Then I realize I have made the same mistake

Tap my feet to the rhythm and blues
And think about those blue suede shoes
I was there when Daltrey broke the news
Play the same music now
But their age laughs at their style

Steve Jacklin

Chapter 11
GLOBAL WAR ON TERRORISM - "*MAGNUM OPUS* "

September 11, 2001: Tuesday was going to be a fun day for all. We had taken a vacation to an east coast beach house in Surf City. We woke at sunrise, walked to the pier, and watched as the sun's orange-colored glare widened and became spherical as it ascended through the horizon. It slowly defined its sizable physique as it climbed into view over the blue ocean of North Carolina. It was placid in its grandeur, bearing witness to its creator.

The weather was typical for the end of a Carolina summer, clear and sunny. The morning painted the sky with a prismatic hue that Tar Heels call "Carolina Blue." A bucolic harmony embraced the dune's tranquility as an FM radio station whispered the melodic tune "One More Day" by Diamond Rio. We knew not then the appropriateness these lyrics would soon have for us.

The temperature was comfortable, absent of the sulfurous Sunbelt humidity. The waves were rolling into the sand, cascading over the foreshore, then retreating in a slow drift, out to the dolphin pod and its cetaceans trolling for breakfast.

Commercial fishermen were busy earning a day's pay as flocks of seagulls hovered over their boats, waiting for chum thrown back into the ocean. A sailboat leisurely skimmed over the glass-like water in search of harmony with the sea. Within hours, the captain of the sloop would be struggling to find equanimity amongst a cataclysm.

On the west side of the Camp Lejeune cantonment area lay the Intracoastal Waterway. The US River and Harbor Act of 1909 established a policy that set in motion the waterway development.

It now starts in Boston and runs the entire east coast of the United States. It's a remarkable engineering feat, illustrative of the quintessential American "can do" attitude and magnificent in its geometry.

As designed from its inception, visiting tourists could see from the front doors of their temporary bungalows boats from as far away as New York meandering their way to Florida or Georgia to Virginia. A conga line of continuous luxurious vessels interspersed with small bass boats making their way along the inland's coastal thoroughfare.

Surf City was a small beach town near the Marine base of Camp Lejeune and its air wing component, New River Air Station.

Because of this geographic proximity, our morning breakfast was treated with an air show. Two AH-1 Cobra attack helicopters made a low pass over the water, strutting their "look at me and my badass machine" silhouette. Moments later, a CH-53 helicopter, colloquially known as a "Shitter," came from the other direction, announcing its arrival by its massive rotor blades vibrating the grave of Chesty Puller (Marine Corp legendary general).

To the novice airman or dilettante, this was better than the San Diego Air Show. Since I had a career in flying Marine aircraft, my thoughts were less enthusiastic.

Unbeknownst to us all, within thirty days, these young aviation warriors would be packing their trash en route to Forward Operating Base Rhino, in a little-known (unless a Kipling fan) shithole country called Afghanistan.

Having just finished a walk on the beach, I was experiencing a casual and relaxed moment, expecting to have a late breakfast, early golf t-time, and an evening at one of Surf City's best seafood emporiums. Then the world came crashing down.

The Journey

The phone rang, and I heard my daughter's voice on the other end, full of angst and trepidation. "Dad, turn on the TV. A plane just crashed into the World Trade Center."

I maintained an outward casual demeanor but lost my relaxed attitude. I turned on the TV. All the channels were tuned into a smoking hole in World Trade Center One, caused by an airplane crashing into the tower at 8:46 a.m. My psyche immediately resembled a duck on water, calm on the surface but paddling like hell underneath.

I began processing the limited information from the newscast. Seeing daily examples of the fake network news wanting to be first not correct, I knew initial reports were usually incomplete or wrong. Don Henley's "Dirty Laundry" song came to mind.

I began a fact-based analysis, starting with *how an airplane could accidentally fly into a building on a clear day?* The mind continued to process—*maybe not an accident, who was piloting the plane, what type of aircraft, and where was its origination airport?*

This critical thinking exercise was interrupted at 9:02 a.m. by a second aircraft crashing into World Trade Center Two. What the fuck! The FBI, CIA, and the rest of our intelligence communities had screwed the pooch. Nineteen Arab terrorists had just pulled off a strike with tactical bravura.

Osama Bin Laden and his chief operations lieutenant, Khalid Sheikh Mohammad, had perfected their *magnum opus,* brilliant in its execution simplicity and victorious in furthering Al Qaida's strategic aspirations.

Seeing the aftermath of the attack on 9/11, along with 300 million other Americans, changed my being. Within forty-eight hours, I was in an active-duty Army uniform supporting the Ohio National Guard's War on Terrorism. Forty-five days later, I was reassigned to the AOC (Army Operations Center) in the Pentagon's basement. Game on!

The Army staffed the AOC with action officers, majors to lieutenant colonels, each with a desk and specific responsibilities. Their job was to track issues, actual or pending, and provide clarity to general officers. The action officers would use all available, classified, and unclassified information to brief Senior Army Staff twice daily, seven days a week.

Mounted on the AOC wall, fifteen feet about the desks of the action officers, were a series of 72 inch TVs. They provided real-time satellite feeds of friendlies on the battlefield, using a system called Blue Force Tracking (BFT). You could watch particular units moving across their operation area, engage the enemy, and maneuver to another target. The BFT provided significant battlefield deconfliction and enhanced clarity within the fog of war.

Abeam the mounted BFT televisions was the balcony. This area of thirty seats allowed the senior Army staff to attend the AOC cadre's twice-daily briefings. The briefs were designed to provide the Secretary of the Army, Chief of Staff of the Army, and other senior staff principles with up-to-date combat situational awareness. The briefs' purpose was twofold: one to enhance senior Army staff's decision-making on resourcing the war, and two, to have a credible answer when a reporter put a microphone in their faces with an ambush interview.

I watched the Pentagon's halls for a roving reporter who would sneak up on general officers in the hallways and attempt to overhear conversations. On more than a few occasions, I reminded the general officer that CNN was within earshot. As if reporters hearing and reporting classified information wasn't bad enough, distorting the reality to fit an agenda was treasonous in a time of war.

The Journey

As an action officer, part of my job was a "backbencher" to provide the general officer with answers during his major presentations and congressional testimonies, providing notes with up-to-date information. You had to have a lot of information at your fingertips to provide your boss with timely and accurate answers.

Arriving in an embattled Washington DC post aerial bombardment, I found it to be surreal. Walking to the Pentagon from my hotel, the surroundings had an atmosphere permeated with the taste of war. The air was putrid with the smell of incinerated concrete, smoke, and fear.

Pentagon 9-11

My hurried walk to the war front would pass anesthetized pedestrians with heads down meandering along with foreboding demeanors. Their hearts seemed heavy, and their faces looked vacuous to the calamity that had occurred.

Closer to the parking lot, the Pentagon came into view. The gaping hole in the "E" Ring of the five-sided edifice was still smoldering as emergency personnel continued to dig through the rubble.

The damaged facade's outer ring was one-fifth headquarters to the world's most incredible fighting machine, now shattered and tattooed with a scorched smoking hole. An occasional muffled emergency vehicle siren could be heard in the distance. *Alaric was at the gates of Rome.*

Elite 82nd Airborne soldiers were omnipresent. Every egress, entrance, and pathway to the building had ubiquitous red beret Jedi's. Six Army tanks were spaced in the parking lot, blocking, funneling, and controlling vehicles. Stinger antiaircraft weapons teams on the Pentagon roof ensured another plane would not crash into the building. Snipers, barely visible amongst the carnage, watched for hostile targets. War had come to the United States.

Within days, we launched airstrikes into Afghanistan. We sent special operators, some on horseback, to Northern Afghanistan to coordinate with the Northern Alliance, the anti-Al Qaida, and anti-Taliban fighters. Within weeks, we secured the entire country, let Osama Bin Laden escape, and started twenty-plus years of nation-building. In the interim, a decision was made to invade another Islamic country.

What about WMD? On one convoy attack south of Bagdad, an IED detonated and destroyed an Army Humvee. The explosion immediately set off the chemical alert. As the rest of the convoy put on their NBC (nuclear, biological, chemical) attire, the battalion chemical officer tried to make sense of what just happened. After close inspection of the IED site, he determined that a 105 Howitzer shell, filled with Sarin gas, was used in the attack. A decision was made at the general officers level to keep this incident quiet should the bad guys realize they had gotten their hands on munitions filled with WMD.

Intercepted Iraqi military communications laid out a plan for Saddam's Republican Guard to tactically deploy an arsenal of biological and chemical weapons should the US invade. The intercepted communications denoted a "red line" drawn south of Bagdad from Karbala to Al Kut. Once the American military

The Journey

crossed this line, the Iraqi field commanders had permission to deploy any or all biological and chemical weapons.

The Pentagon took this intel seriously and ordered ten thousand body bags delivered to the invading American forces. Of course, Saddam was bluffing, holding black Aces and Eights. Next to Wild Bill Hickok, Saddam was one of the unluckiest poker players ever to play that hand.

With the US Iraq invasion buildup, we watched a convoy of Russian trucks leaving Central Iraq heading for Syria on satellite in the Pentagon. The consensus was Saddam was moving his WMD cache out of the country. The trucks were off-limits to our bombers due to the possibility of killing the Russian drivers. There was no direct evidence to support the WMD movement theory, but Syrian Dictator Assad used WMD on his people during the Syrian Civil War. Smart people could easily draw a straight line of WMD from Baghdad to Damascus.

Iraq Patrol

I needed to "ride to the sound of the cannons," and in the summer of 2006, I went to Iraq for the Defense Logistics Agency. I moved right into the storm center, Ramadi and Fallujah. I worked on weapon systems for the Army and Marines, ensuring the logistic flow continued, keeping weapons systems up and ready. I found overwhelming destructive chaos, carnage, and death, void of any possible solutions.

Not all was fire and brimstone. I met some great guys. Most were against the war but still performed at a high level of professionalism with some comical overtones.

The Alamo Iraq

Bernard was one of the younger "hombres" in our clique, African-American from Chicago, personable and pushing the ripe old age of 32. One morning, around 2 a.m., the warning siren went off, signaling an incoming mortar attack. We quickly left our hooches and began running to the bunker for shelter. I busted ass out of my door and almost collided with Bernard. He was hauling ass out of his hooch with a half-shit-eating grin on his face.

As we ran to the shelter, Bernard kept sounding the clarion call "Gooks in the wire, gooks in the wire." I tumbled over with laughter.

After a few stumbles, Bernard and I were safe inside the bunker. I turned and, with a curious tone, said to this youngster, "Hey man, you're not old enough to have been in Vietnam; what's with the gooks in the wire shout-out?"

Firfight Iraq

He laughed and said his dad was a Nam Vet and would always use the phase when something would go wrong. He said his dad would also shout "grenade" whenever he would drop something. He said his dad eventually stopped the grenade shout-out when Iraq and Afghanistan veterans started to come back home. He didn't want to excite any PTSD episode.

We had a good laugh, and when the mortar attack was over, we did a fist bump and went back to our hooches to finish our night's sleep. No harm, no foul.

I left Iraq in February 2007 with the war's outcome still in doubt.

TO WHAT END HAVE WE BEEN

The guns lay silent on the hill
Gravestone ripe with daffodils
Ne'er the voice a mother's shrill
To what end have we been

Spoken as a moralist
Echoes from the Eucharist
Forgiveness for the pugilist
To what end have we been

Hear the cry pick up the sword
Strap on the sheath join the horde
Do battle in G minor chord
To what end have we been

Tracked and brawled with Bedouin
Galvanize the frequent winds
Wake up and load inside the tin
To what end have we been

Steve Jacklin

Smell the heated painted metal
Engulf by fire the drive be fatal
Shut my eyes and see the devil
To what end have we been

Bring the flag draped basket back
Precision steps on black tarmac
Hear the whimpers and faux facts
To what end have we been

Now the home a brownish berth
The voices sing for all it's worth
I cry out loud with pain and hurt
To what end have we been

Chapter 11A
THE POLITICS OF GWOT – *"IF THIS WAS EASY, THE FRENCH WOULD BE DOING IT"*

While we were killing the Randy Weaver family, being entertained by the spectacle of the OJ trial, focusing on the white militia, burning Waco inhabitants, and impeaching a president, the Fedayeen adroitly morphed into an effective killing machine called Al Qaida.

While President Bill Clinton was being distracted by young female interns in the Oval Office, the country ignored countless warnings and failed to take action, and now we were paying a heavy price.

As early as 1998, there was intelligence chatter about using commercial airplanes as weapons. Our intelligence community's hubris discarded these possibilities and focused on traditional attacks; vehicle-borne bombs, airplane hijacking, ransom kidnappings, and assassinations.

The government apparatus we set up to ensure the nation's security had become a bureaucratic behemoth that perpetuated interdepartmental jealousies, territorial disputes, and fear-mongering to seize more of the congressional budget.

We failed to heed Pearl Harbor's lessons, the surprise 1968 Tet Offensive in Vietnam, the 1983 Beirut Barracks Bombing, and the attack on the USS Cole docked in Aden, Yemen, October 2000.

Additionally, an intelligence breakdown occurred in 1995 that was never fixed. Domestic terrorist Timothy McVeigh destroyed the Alfred P. Murrah Building in Oklahoma City. He murdered over 160 innocent men, women, and children with only forty bags of commercial fertilizer and a rented Ryder truck. The attack was brilliant in its execution, simplicity and highlighted the incompetence of our intelligence community.

I supported the invasion of Iraq. The intelligence reports we received in the Pentagon seemed to justify the war. Saddam Hussein was supporting, at least passively, Ansar al-Islam, an Al Qaeda surrogate. Saddam developed, possessed, and used chemical weapons on his citizens, the Kurds. Iraq's army also used Sarin and mustard gas on Iranian forces during the Iraq/Iran intermural battles.

Nothing the UN inspection team reported indicated Iraq's WMD had been destroyed or removed from its arsenal. The fear was Saddam would provide his gas and biological weapons to other terrorist groups bent on attacking the US.

The Neo-Con's sent Bush's Secretary of State Colin Powell to the United Nations to pitch the Iraq invasion. He was the point man for the US war. Powell brought with him an array of photos, audio conversations, and a stellar reputation. His presentation to the organization's General Assembly was convincing and credible. But as we would find out later, his "sale pitch" to the UN was as genuine as a used car salesman trying to unload a '65 Corvair.

General Powell's charismatic performance to the community of nations was the catalyst that launched our country into a tragedy.

His cloaked reputation would surface and come to light as a faux persona, void of integrity, saturated with plenary notoriety. The far-left would designate Powell a war criminal. I wouldn't go that far but would say he lacked a moral compass. Like SecDef McNamara of the Vietnam War, Colin Powell sent men and women into harm's way, knowing the conflict would not generate a positive outcome.

During the First Gulf War, Powell was Chairman of the Joint Chiefs of Staff. His counsel to George H. W. Brush was not to remove Saddam and occupy Iraq after the US quick Kuwait victory. The logic behind this course of action was twofold; removing the Dictator would provide a power vacuum in the region. Two, it would empower Iran to move into this power vacuum. In 1991, Powell subscribed to the *Pottery Barn Rule*, "If you break it, you own it." Over the next fifteen years, General Powell's philosophy would morph him into a racial medieval cottar.

The best illustration of this was his overt and public support for Barrack Obama's 2008 election. After selling the Iraq invasion's propriety and rightness to the UN, sending over 500,000 men and women into harm's way, he then abandoned those military warriors. He supported Obama over the president he served, George W. Bush, and longtime friend John McCain. He would align with Barack Obama and against the invasion he championed.

Obama's 2008 cornerstone campaign platform was how disastrous the decision to invade Iraq was, how corrupt the Bush Administration was to launch the war with lies of WMD, and how inept and criminal the conduct and performance of our troops were. Barack referred to our troops as terrorists committing war crimes. I took these screeds personally.

So why did Colin Powell change course and his support for Bush's war policy, thus altering his opinion of the war he aggressively championed?

One simple reason, **the tribalism of race**. Powell threw away a lifetime of voting his conscience, putting what's right for his country, and decided to vote the color of one's skin.

Powell's "race vote" would bring to mind an MLK quote "There is nothing more tragic than to find an individual bogged down in the length of life, devoid of breadth."

I supported W due to his aggressive war on terrorism. Bush used all the tools of the government, with the sole priority of keeping Americans safe. His strategy was truculent, thorough, and effective in preventing further planned major terrorist attacks on the Homeland.

But my post-9/11 attitude toward Bush's presidency evolved as the calendar moved forward. Time allows an unvarnished context to assess the reality of past moments, becoming more focused as the facts become clearer and the opinion changes. History will not judge President George W. Bush kindly. With his debacle in Iraq, failed leadership with Hurricane Katrina, the unwieldy "No Child Left Behind" education bureaucracy, expansion of federal government with Medicare Part D, creation of a police state with the Patriot Act, and falling asleep as the 2008 financial market collapsed communicates history's notice to a failed presidency.

Even longer-lasting and more harmful to the Republic was W's appointment of the Kafkaesque character John Roberts to SCOTUS. Bush's appointment of Judge Roberts was an "apical dendrite" of a mediocre Administration.

The Global War on Terrorism (GWOT) met its primary goal of keeping American cities safe but not without significant lasting mistakes.

The GWOT had bipartisan support in Congress, with public support for action against Iraq. Politicians and "talking head" media cretins painted a quick invasion and a smooth transition with Iraqis support and gratitude.

The Department of Defense had a less jaded attitude about the incursion. When I was asked my assessment of the pending invasion, I would quip, *"if this were easy, the French would be doing it."*

Secretary Donald Rumsfeld was a **good** Secretary of Defense (SecDef). But as is often said about him, he was a **great** Secretary of War. Having served as a Naval Aviator and whose father served in the Pacific during WWII, he knew the human cost of sending troops into combat. He would always challenge the popular assumptions, asking for secondary and tertiary effects.

During the final planning stage of OIF (Operation Iraqi Freedom), the Pentagon Operations Center received a memo from the office of SecDef. The title of the memo was *Parade of Horribles (see essay)*.

Rumsfeld had 29 issues he wanted to be addressed by Pentagon staffers. He demanded an assessment of the probability of happening and the fallout should any one of the 29 Horribles happen. He wanted answers to the known unknowns and demanded critical thinking beyond the course de jure.

Along with critical thinking of the effects of an invasion of a Muslim country, Rumsfeld was in a constant battle with the neo-cons (John Bolton, Paul Wolfowitz, Elliot Abrams, Richard Perle, etc.) and the Military-Industrial Complex. They all wanted a full-scale invasion with a footprint of over 250,000 troops and a lengthy occupation of Iraq's oil fields.

Additionally, the SecDef was at odds with some of the general officer corps; I called the intra-palisade skirmishes "Clinton's Generals, Rumsfeld's War." They would often undermine the DOD approach by leaking to the press or retiring and writing tell-all books.

General Eric Ken Shinseki, The Army Chief of Staff, appeared to be continually battling with Rumsfeld. Shinseki fired the first verbal volley in June 2001 when SecDef Rumsfeld directed the services to restructure its force and operating concepts to be in line with the current threat. Since the USSR's fall in 1990, the military strategy was still fighting a war with the Soviets. Weapons systems were still developing on the procurement calendar, with significant cost overruns and schedule delays. Even though the USSR collapsed ten years earlier, the Swamp and the military-industrial complex were still planning for the Red Storm Rising; big profits fighting the Soviets.

Shinseki wasn't the only "Clinton General" pushing back on strategy and modernization but was certainly the loudest and the most public. These quarrels would filter down to the enlisted and officer corps in the Pentagon, adding confusion and disarray to the warfighters.

In addition to clashes over modernization, Rumsfeld canceled two weapon systems. The Crusader, a self-propelled howitzer system with a price tag of over 11 billion dollars. The project lacked mobility and proven accuracy. The behemoth system weighed 110 tons with its supply trailer, too heavy to be transported by a C-5 Galaxy.

The second of Shinseki's sacred cows was the RAH-66 Comanche helicopter. After twenty years in development with schedule delays and cost overruns, the developer could not determine the Comanche project completion date or final cost. During a 2002 review, the system cost was $26 billion and counting. In 2004, the SecDef moved to cancel the Comanche Program.

In the six years of Rummy's SecDef tenure, he was able to shit can several "Clinton Generals." Unfortunately, getting rid of the malcontent civilian Senior Executive Service staff, later known as the "Swamp," was almost impossible.

Once the war turned ugly, the *summer soldier and the sunshine patriot* pounded the daily news cycle with the mantra and chyron's of no planning or "ineffective managing the war efforts." The talking heads knew not what they were speaking, and career officers would leak to the press a mantra of recalcitrance to ensure their fingerprints were not on the war planning or execution.

The invasion's turning point with the news media was the declaration of *"an end to major combat operations in Iraq"* by President Bush aboard the aircraft carrier, USS Abraham Lincoln. The ship's captain hung a banner reading MISSION ACCOMPLISHED just below the ship's Pri-Fly. The banner's purpose was to acknowledge the accomplishment of the crew of the Abe Lincoln. They had fulfilled their mission and were going home, a BRAVO ZULU; job well done. The fake news spun this as Bush declared the Iraq War over. As we would later see, this certainly wasn't the case, and the drive-by news media would attack and beat W repeatedly with the MISSION ACCOMPLISHED banner photo op.

The required declaration, *"end to major combat operations in Iraq,"* was necessary diplomatic verbiage that allowed a transition point in the invasion. Bush's adage was a trigger that turned authority over from the Department of Defense occupation force to the US State Department. Ambassador Paul Bremer was now at the helm, calling the shots.

During the first few months of the occupation, Bremer made a series of mistakes that would affect peace and security in the region. The first mistake was to disband the Iraqi army. This dismantling plan put thousands of young Iraqi soldiers out of work, no job, no money, pissed off.

The second major mistake was to fire senior Iraqi generals, leaving them to ferment and lead an insurgency, primarily from the unemployed pissed-off soldiers.

The third major mistake was to shut down the Ba'ath Party and fire any member of the organization that was an active member or government official of the party during Saddam's regime. These were the technocrats that kept the lights on and the water running.

These miscalculations would facilitate Iraq's plunge into chaos and destructions, allowing the insurgency to metastasize.

In 2006, General George Casey was commanding the Multi-National Forces in Iraq. By all accounts, he was a quality officer, respected by this peers and soldiers, but lacked a warrior mindset to finish the war. More of an administrator than a fighter.

I found he surrounded himself with pogue (non-warrior staff) senior bureaucrats, noted for their focus on petty bullshit and prevent defense instead of aggressive execution of the war. Case in point, Casey's Command Sergeant Major, was more concerned with troops wearing their hats and saluting in the field than operating safely around M-1 tanks, getting troops fed, or killing bad guys. He was not of the warrior ilk, lacking respect from the soldiers and officers who would speak derisively about him.

Luckily for the war effort, General Dave Petraeus took command, built a quality team, and commanded "The Surge" in 2007. He built a team of fighters and planners who thought outside the box with an aggressive winning mindset. He had exceptional leadership skills that the local Iraqi Sunnis appreciated. On every level, Petraeus successfully executed "The Surge" counter-insurgency plan. Success and relative peace ensued in Iraq. Petraeus was a top-notch warrior. If he could have kept his libido in check, he would have been the Eisenhower or Omar Bradley of our day.

I settled into my later years with a certain uneasiness about where the Global War on Terrorism was going. My disquietude stemmed from President Obama's sycophantic behavior toward Iran and the Administration's execution of the terrorist fight.

Cozying up to the world's number one sponsor of terrorism, Iran, was problematic. The American people's vote for Obama in 2008 put into motion a failed Middle East strategy. Barack Hussain Obama's reelected in 2012 reaffirmed his position as an Ayatollah quisling and caused me further angst as to where the country was heading.

As a result of my frustrations with the voter's 2008 and 2012 decisions, I postulated a manifesto of my last 50 years; "At 18 I wanted to change the world. At 33 I was angry I couldn't change the world. At 70, fuck it, it's not my problem anymore".

I passed the baton to the next generation. The United States is a great country and will continue to be a great county only if the young remain vigilant and proactive in striving to live up to our founding fathers' promises;

- Equality of opportunity, not equality of outcome.
- A Republic built on the rule of law.
- See a person for the content of his character, not the color of his skin.
- Inalienable rights come from God, not a central government.
- The US Constitution is the single most important document in the history of government.

Warning; while we neutralize the terrorist from abroad, don't fall asleep to the institutional terrorist within.

C-117 moves on
planes wheels up fly into sky
Rapid fall now entombed

Women wrapped in blue rags
Future now is their yesterday
Wife twelve year old girl

Bagram is no more
Eighty billion dollars lost
We give you our guns

Steve Jacklin

Al Qaida is home
Resurrect the terror beast
Suburban mom ruins

Count the huddle mass
Sequences who is to pass
Explode the thirteen

System faked election
We now own the consequence
Carnage three more years

Who is now in charge
Border inflation terror
God I missed those tweets

Essay on THE DEEP STATE and the SWAMP CREATURES

A significant accomplishment of Donald J. Trump's presidency was to expose three realities living in American cultural governance, the liberal corrupt media, the Deep State, and Swamp Creatures.

The Deep State is a descriptive term for the operational architect of the US government. Its primary effect is on the federal side but overlaps with state and local administrations when political alignment is warranted. The Deep State inhabitants can thwart the "will of the masses" through indirect control or government policy and direct manipulation of the power apparatus.

The Deep State employs Swamp Creatures to act as enforcers, targeting identified heretics or non-believer and ensuring neutralization of those apostates.

The Swamp Creatures are partisan career civil servant technocrats and political appointees. Their goal is to further the partisan agenda and to ensure the status quo is maintained. The Swampers ensure equilibrium within the Deep State.

Having seen the Swamp Creatures in action throughout my adult military and civilian executive career was troubling. However, seeing significant efforts to maintain power by destroying a president and his agenda was nightmarish in its overtones.

I flashbacked to the government corruption and misconduct brought to light by the 1975 bipartisan Senate investigation into the levers of US power. The Church Committee (formally the United States Senate Select Committee to Study Governmental Operations With Respect to Intelligence Activities) was a US Senate select committee in 1975 that investigated abuses by the Central Intelligence Agency (CIA), National Security Agency (NSA), Federal Bureau of Investigation (FBI), and the Internal Revenue Service (IRS). The Commission found the Deep State to be deep, corruption rampant, and abuse of power a routine operating procedure.

A look back to some earlier experiences with the Deep State presents a disturbed, dysfunctional picture. Some examples to follow.

The country began the 21 Century partying like it was 1999, to paraphrase Prince. We were in a tailspin with concerns over global computer systems collapsing. The scare was called the Y2K Bug, a computer flaw (or faux) that would cause massive IT disruptions and a societal breakdown as computer systems operating with dates beyond December 31, 1999, would not run.

If it came to fruition, the perceived computer malady would shut down all computers on the globe, stopping cars, shutting down hospital heart transplants in progress, airplanes falling out of the sky, and microwave ovens failing, leaving your Hot Pockets soggy.

The global community spent billions of dollars upgrading legacy computers and any equipment with a computer chip in its functional design. Consultants, IT companies, and a select number of Swamp Creatures, mostly congressional hacks that appropriated the Y2K fix it budget, made a fortune.

The Ohio Army National Guard Staff spent midnight, 2000, on high alert at State Headquarters awaiting the pending collapse of civilization.

As the computer clock rolled to 1201, the desktop computers kept running. The mainframe computers were still processing. The NASA Space Network was still communicating with the Hubble telescope via computerized satellites. WTF!

CNN had been hard at work the last year promoting the impending collapse of our information processing systems. Now, it was hard at work covering their ass, making excuses for their orgy of fake Y2K news stories they prematurely ejaculated over cable news the past 12 months.

At 0800, the operations officer briefed the Ohio Governor that all was well. The National Guard Staff had, again, walked the state back from the ledge of civilizations collapse, thus saving the world for democracy. What horse shit!

Having not slept for two days, I went home and crashed for eight hours. When I awoke, I immediately printed a box of business cards with a bold letter heading **Y3K** and the tagline, ***never too early to start planning***. I was making sure I got a piece of the action with the next bogus calamity.

This episode would add to my jaded myopic viewpoint of world events, the media, and government proclamations. I mentally filed this away with other fabricated incidents; The Gulf of Tonkin Resolution, the need for the Patriot Act, the WMD invasion of Iraq, the Russian Hoax in the 2016 election, COVID19. Joe Biden became president by getting more African-American votes in 2020 than Barack Obama did in his elections. Was 2020 a statistical anomaly or orchestrated fraud? Vladimir Putin couldn't pull off those electoral numbers.

My cataloging of these fake events added to a mindset that solidified a belief that the "Swamp" was literal and active in the Deep State.

The Deep State became hyperactive during the Trump Administration, employing every tool it had to diminish, weaken and destroy his presidency.

It was not a new phenomenon, with a part of governmental stewardship since early institutional conception. Over three thousand years ago, Egyptian Pharaoh Akhenaten was stymied by the priesthood class due to his decree for a monotheist deity. The motivation for the priest class' disapproval was less pious altruism and more self-interest, as is the case with the operations of most Deep State actors.

When Akhenaten disbanded the priesthoods of all their polytheist gods, he stripped them of their power and diverted the income from those cults to support his monotheists. Similar to today's Swamp Creatures jostling for power and money.

He was not successful in his battle with the Deep State apparatus. During his reign, the empire began its precipitous decline, primarily due to the Swamp Creators undermining his edicts and rulings, overloading the system, hence collapsing the governing apparatus (reference Cloward and Piven)

The Deep State's presents prompted leaders to try and enact a counterbalance. Roman emperors had their Praetorian Guard, and medieval royalty depended on the church to buttress their crown against deep state renegades. George Washington had Alexander Hamilton, John Kennedy had Bobby, and Sonny had Cher.

The Third Reich's Deep State had "brown shirts" used by Hitler's Ministry of Propaganda, Joseph Goebbels. These Swamp Creatures would enforce the censoring of information, control the narrative, and ensure the Nazi message was the only message presented to the masses, not unlike today's "mainstream" media and big tech. Stray from the accepted narrative, and the Deep State will come crashing down on you.

The US has its embedded structure of the Deep State, often described as the fourth branch of government, **called administrative**. As the central government grew in size, regulatory authority, and power, the Deep State grew more entrenched, territorial, and self-serving, a concern Thomas Jefferson, Patrick Henry, James Madison, and other founding fathers would foresee.

The organizational psychology of the Deep State can be explained by following the fundamental laws of physics. Newton's law of universal gravitation states that "the gravitational pull of any object is proportional to the object's size." This metaphysically applies to the government. The larger it gets, the more its self-survival instance kicks in, with more gravitational pull exerted with one purpose, to ensure power remains in the hands of a selected few.

The gravitational pull of the enlarged Deep State will be propositional to the danger it perceives, diminishing its power. Every task performed is focused on keeping the status quo and self-perpetuating the organization. No outsiders allowed, no changes to what has been working for the last 75 years.

We can also apply Newton's law of motion to organizational theory. This law states, "An object will remain at rest.... unless acted upon by an external force." The organization is the object at rest, and its physical nature is to remain at rest, status quo.

Newton's third law states, "When one body exerts a force on a second body, the second body simultaneously exerts a force equal in magnitude and opposite in direction on the first body." If an outside force or interloper enters the sphere of the first body, the Deep State will simultaneously apply pressure to either neutralize or destroy the intruder.

In 2015, Donald J. Trump, an interloper, exerted an external force acting upon a body at rest (status quo), causing the organization to exert forces equal or greater in magnitude in the opposite direction.

The gravity of the pull in the opposite direction is proportional to the size of the government. The Swamp Creatures had a force multiplier by weaponizing the FBI, CIA, DOJ, IRS, NSC, and State Department to ensure no one could disrupt, clean up or eliminate the waste, fraud, and abuse within the Deep State. The Swamp must maintain the power levers it groomed over decades, ensure the organizational structure was aroused by the perceived upstart, and destroy any attempt at reform the outsider is trying.

The Deep State will use procedures, regulations, and existing statutes to dismantle any outside control or investigations attempt. If these tactics are unable to keep the status quo, the Deep State will weaponize more aggressive tools of government against its perceived threat.

The weaponized branches of the Deep State act like white blood cells in the human immune system, working to destroy any infection.

The factors that make up the Deep State can be bundled into four baskets, government, corporations, businesses, and the 5th Estate. These enterprises can work independently but often work in concert with each other to amplify their effectiveness. No mission statement, written plan, or zoom meeting to coordinate their efforts. Only a shared ideology and a willingness driven toward an implicit goal of self-perpetuation.

The Deep State institution of government includes the federal, state, and local principalities. These systems seldom work in tandem, given our system of federalism and territorial jealously, but frequently have parallel systems in place mirroring each other's operations that overlap, particularly in the area of money transitions. These governance fiefdoms have built internal investigative tools, public relations machines, political apparatus, and collegial "logrolling" systems that stretch back generations.

The operation of these entities is governed by Newton's first law of inertia, the tendency to remain at rest unless acted upon by an external force. Whether a political scandal or an outsider gaining unchecked power, the external pressure will prompt the system to apply Newton's third law of action and reaction. If a body (external force) exerts a force on a second body (Deep State), the Swamp and cohorts simultaneously exert a force equal to or greater in magnitude in the opposite direction on the first body.

The tools to apply equal or greater force in magnitude can take various forms, Saul Alinsky's Rules for Radicals, Vladimir

Lenin's recruitment of UI's (Useful Idiots), Richard Nixon's White House Plumbers, Bill Clintons War Room, and Obama's Insurance Policy to name a few. The external forces are continually at work to maintain the equilibrium and not change the body politics, with the Deep State constantly on guard for unwelcome interlopers.

A few examples of Government Swamp Creatures are as follows:

The US State Department. Employees model themselves after the bureaucratic system of the British Empire. The Brits successfully maintained a vast empire by building a cadre of non-elected professional administrators managing departments. The administrators were selected by a meritocratic system of education and testing.

Today, the US State Department is staffed by opportunistic Ivy League graduates and political appointments, usually getting their positions as payback from the party bosses.

The bureaucracy is deep, with loyalties to the system, not the head of the department or the people's elected president. Career employees at Foggy Bottom derisively refer to the incoming administration as the "Summer Help," knowing policies put in place by a new administration can be forestalled or ignored until a new Chief Executive is elected in four years. Their gall and hubris are constantly on display.

The US Intelligence Community. The CIA has been at odds with an open society since its inception, post-WWII. By nature, the Agency is secretive and deceptive. One of the CIA's primary tools is to classify everything and refuse to submit to congressional oversight anything that has a classification.

In 1975, the CIA, FBI, and the NSA were exposed by the Church Commission, a bipartisan congressional committee that brought thirty years of secretive misdeeds to light. From the 1953

Iranian coup of Mohammad Mosaddegh to the overthrow of the elected president of Chile, Salvador Allende, in 1973, Congress appeared to be surprised and outraged by these actions.

After the Church commission's exposure and subsequent regulatory revisions, the CIA presumably played by the book while submerging and making itself more recondite into the Deep State. They would become more aligned with the technocrats in the US State Department.

Post 9/11 overhaul changed the rules and decreased congressional oversight requirements. As a result of a congress's lack of oversight and a deeper dive into the Deep State, the CIA and the State Department felt comfortable setting up a gun-running scheme with the Free Syrian Army (FSA). The operation had the passive approval of Secretary of State Hillary Clinton. It was managed out of the Libyan consulate in Benghazi in concert with a CIA annex three blocks away, under anyone's radar.

When shit hit the fan and Ansar al-Sharia attacked the consulate, the Deep State immediately launched a panoply of tools it had at the ready. The media assumed its protective posture to the administration, the political apparatus went into destructive personal attacks, and the Intel Community refused comments due to classified information.

A tried and true tactic, known as circular reporting, was employed. With selective leaks to the media, the media would report on the leaks. The Swamp actors reference the leaked media reports as evidence of their claims. The media then reported the Deep State actor's press briefing using the leaked media reports as evidence.

With the circular reporting complete, the Deep State relies on the UI (Useful Idiots) to only read the chyron and internet news headlines and build the disinformation campaign.

FBI. The FBI will hide behind three factors, (1) will not comment on an open investigation, (2) the Foreign Intelligence Surveillance Act (FISA) that authorizes a secret court to bypass the 4th, 6th, and 14th Amendments of the US Constitution. FISA court also suspends habeas corpus. The public wrongly assumes the secret Foreign Intelligence Surveillance Court (FISC) was a post 9/11 construct. In reality, it was put into place by Congress in 1978 to the Church Commission findings to ensure congressional oversight into the governments' surveillance activities by the CIA, FBI, and NSA. Instead, the FISA process has morphed and evolved into a Deep State tool to ensure the Swamp can act unobstructed without oversight.

The third (3) factor is the organizational structure of the FBI and its self-promotional opportunities. The FBI director (highest-ranking position in the FBI) is appointed by the president for a 10-year term and confirmed by the US Senate. The FBI is structured under the Department of Justice but remains detached from the Executive branch, at least in theory.

One fundamental promotional practice within the FBI I call "The monkey move-up." It allows a domino promotion sequence. The election of 2016 is a perfect example. To the surprise of the Deep State, Hillary Clinton lost to Trump, with her election defeat upsetting the monkey move-up within DOJ and FBI.

Every investigation of Clinton's lawlessness was circular filed (wastebasket) and not acted upon. The Swamp needed to ensure that once Hillary was elected, they would be rewarded with promotions. To ensure this, they refused to investigate the supposed next president-elect.

This is how "The monkey move-up" was going work; Loretta Lynch, the AG, would get a seat on the Supreme Court. James Comey, the FBI Director, would become the next AG under a Hillary Administration. Andrew McCabe, Comey's assistance, would move up to Director FBI. Peter Strzok, the investigator that "deep-sixed" the Hillary investigation, would take McCabe's place, and so on, The MONKEY MOVE UP! The only problem, Trump got elected and fucked up the whole domino motility.

Once Donald J. Trump was elected the 45 President, the plotters, planners, and Deep State operatives went to work to ensure enough smoke and chaos were introduced into the Trump Administration to ensure maximum self-preservation. The goal was to prevent discovering any subterfuge, malfeasance, and conspiracy of the Swamp creators. Now enters the Russian Hoax and fake Putin's interference in the 2016 election.

The fake news media picked up the mantra and carried the water for the Democrats, the left, and the Never Trumpers. The conservative media would use the phrase "Coup de estate" or "Conspiracy to remove a duly elected president." But the Russian Hoax's actual reasoning was simply an attempt by the Swamp to cover their ass as to the intended "Monkey move up." They planned to run out the clock till a new administration was in office. This was achieved by adding confusion, disinformation, and continuous fake news propaganda.

The FBI and DOJ would facilitate this cover-up, not for any complicity but because that's the way the Deep State works, loyalty to its organization, not the law. Today, not one Deep State actor has seen jail time in what would be a lengthy prison stay for a private citizen guilty of the same offense.

Media and Corporations. Other opportunists have secured a place in the Deep State. Profiteers have joined the party in search of quarterly profits. From corporate media like Comcast, Disney, and AT&T, these profiteers have published incendiary headlines and fake news to gain internet clicks and increase quarterly revenue. The country's best interest be damned. Business enterprises like the NBA, Nike, the Chamber of Commerce put a larger Chinese market over the well beings of American businesses and middle-class jobs.

Nike has a 4-billion-dollar market share in the US but a 35-billion-dollar market share in China. Nike overlooks slave labor, environmental issues, and workplace safety to ensure part of the 1.6 billion Chinese wear Nike Waffle Racers 2X tennis shoes; Lebron James needs another 20.5 million dollar mansion.

Loyalty to the American people that built these entities has been replaced by a desire to embrace a market populated by billions of Southeast Asian consumers. By using slave labor for cheap tennis shoes

the Swamp Creatures of the Deep State will ensure nothing upsets this profit center.

The 5th Estate. The internet boom of the 1990s laid the groundwork for what we call social media today. A more dated term is the 5th Estate, first used with the 1960 counterculture. It referred to a socio-cultural grouping of outlier viewpoints in contemporary society, manifesting itself with underground newspapers and pamphlets.

The term comes from expanding the classical reference to three estates of the realm, clergy, nobility, and commoner. The 4th Estate is the mainstream media, and the 5th Estate has mutated into Big Tech, i.e., Google, Twitter, Facebook, etc.

Today we have a monopoly on information platforms provided by the 5th Estate; the oligarchs controlling these behemoths censor, control, and direct us down the information highway. Since most world citizens receive their news from internet clicks, they often are fed misinformation and fake news. History has recorded numerous disasters precipitated by control and dissemination of misinformation (Iraq WMD). The potential for the 5th Estate to control elections, corrupt government actions, and organize community disruptions is dangerous.

So why have we not taken action to address the issue? Simple, political graft in the form of political campaign donations, corporate patronage, and nepotism.

The billion-dollar Big Tech monopolies funnel millions of dollars to our elected congressional members to ensure regulations do not interfere with profit. As a quid pro quo, the Big Tech oligarchs ensure only the information paid for by politicians are processed through their algorithms, continually providing disinformation to UI's that get only snapshots of cultural happenings.

In this world of today, significant obstacles have been erected to our constitutional republic. The genius of James Madison's remarkable document is being diluted. The 13 original states would require a Bill of Rights (first ten amendments to the US Constitution) before ratifying the US Constitution. The Bill of Rights was well thought out and provided an addendum to Madison's masterwork. But the tenets of the constitutions Bill of Rights have been under attack, eroding faith in the rule of law and providing a two-tiered justice system.

The Bill of Rights is purposely ignored, debased, bastardized, and politicized by attacks from the courts, media, academia, and the Deep State. From free speech (1st Amendment) being castigated, gun rights being taken away (2nd Amendment), and unreasonable search and seizure (3d Amendment), the attack is staggering.

The Deep State has used the tools of government to spy on individuals, including a sitting president (4th Amendment). The government continually abuses individual rights (5th Amendment), trial delays for political prisoners, negating the requirement for a speedy trial (6th Amendment).

Trial by a jury of peers (7th Amendment) has been replaced with jury and judge shopping. No excessive bail (8th Amendment) has given cause for a release with no bail of criminals running amok in major cities.

The citizens have rights not listed in the constitution (9th Amendment) but are revoked by state and local governments.

The US Constitution gave the federal government only 18 enumerated powers but added a clause "Necessary and Proper." This clause would give the federal government unlimited power to control its citizens (10 Amendment). Note: Alexander Hamilton cited and used this authority for establishing the first national bank.

A clarion call has been sounded. The Tea Party started the revolution but was curtailed by the Deep State's IRS. Then Trump was shockingly inaugurated as the 45 President of the United States. Even though the election initially stymied the Deep State, it quickly gained its battle footing and assumed an offensive posture. The Swamp is now employed to execute the counter-revolution.

The mind, once enlightened, cannot again become dark.
Thomas Paine

Whenever the people are well-informed, they can be trusted with their own government.
Thomas Jefferson

An oppressive government is more to be feared than a tiger.
Confucius

Only virtuous people are capable of freedom. As nations become corrupt and vicious, they have more need of masters.
Benjamin Franklin

Steve Jacklin

When there is a lack of honor in government, the morals of the whole people are poisoned.
                                                        Herbert Hoover

A patriot must always be ready to defend his country against his government.
                                                          Edward Abbey

A government big enough to give you everything you need is a government big enough to take away everything you have.
                                                       Thomas Jefferson

Iraq's *Parade of Horribles*

During the 2002 planning for the invasion of Iraq, Secretary of Defense Donald Rumsfeld directed the Pentagon staffers to think "outside of the box" on the repercussions of the invasion. He titled his memo to all staff, The *Parade of Horribles*. Rumsfeld listed 29 issues with the invasion and occupation of Iraq. He required all 29 issues to be analyzed, addressing each item's probability of happening and postulating a mitigation strategy for all 29.

Invading Iraq was an ill-advised foreign venture, but the planning for the invasion was detailed and well thought out. What could not be quantified was the *known unknowns*. What was not qualified was Middle East stability and the erosion of America's psyche.

Here are Rumsfeld's *Parade of Horribles:*
1. If the US seeks UN approval, it could fail; and without a UN mandate, potential coalition partners may be unwilling to participate.
2. A failure to answer this question could erode support: "If the US pre-empts in one country, does it mean it will pre-empt in all other terrorist states?"
3. The US could fail to restrain Israel, and if Israel entered the conflict, it could broaden into a Middle East war.
4. Syria and Iran could decide to support Iraq, complicating the war.
5. Turkish military could move on the Kurds or the Northern Iraqi oil fields.

6. The Arab street could erupt, particularly if the war is long, destabilizing friendly countries neighboring Iraq—Jordan, Saudi Arabia, DC states, Pakistan, etc.
7. While the US is engaged in Iraq, another rogue state could take advantage of US preoccupation—North Korea, Iran, PRC in the Taiwan Straits, others.
8. While preoccupied with Iraq, the US might feel compelled to ignore serious proliferation or other machinations by North Korea, Russia, PRC, Pakistan, India, etc., and thereby seem to tacitly approve and acquiesce in unacceptable behavior, to the detriment of US influence in the world.
9. Preoccupation with Iraq for a long period could lead to US inattentiveness and diminished influence in South Asia, which could lead to a conflict between nuclear-armed states.
10. Oil disruption could cause international shock waves, and with South America already in distress.
11. Iraqi intelligence services, which have a global presence, including in the US, could strike the US, our allies, and/or deployed forces in unconventional ways.
12. Countries will approach the US with unexpected demands in exchange for their support (an Israeli request for us to release Jonathan Pollard, Russia asking for free play in the Pankisi Gorge, etc.), which, if the US accepts, will weaken US credibility.
13. US could fail to find WAD on the ground in Iraq and be unpersuasive to the world.
14. There could be higher-than-expected collateral damage—Iraqi civilian deaths.
15. There could be higher-than-expected US and coalition deaths from Iraq's use of weapons of mass destruction against coalition forces in Iraq, Kuwait, and/or Israel.

16. The US could fail to find Saddam Hussein and face problems similar to the difficulty in not finding him. BULL [Osama bin Laden] and [Mullah] Omar.
17. The US could fail to manage post-Saddam Hussein Iraq successfully, with the result that it could fracture into two or three pieces, to the detriment of the Middle East and the benefit of Iran.
18. The dollar cost of the effort could prove to be greater than expected, and the contributions from other nations minimal.
19. Rather than having the post-Saddam effort require two to four years, it could take eight to 10 years, thereby absorbing US leadership, military, and financial resources.
20. US alienation from countries in the EU and the UN could grow to levels sufficient to make our historic post-World War II relationships irretrievable, with the charge of US unilateralism becoming so embedded in the world's mind that it leads to a diminution of US influence in the world.
21. US focus on Iraq could weaken our effort in the Global War on Terrorism, leading to terrorist attacks against the US or Europe, including a WMD attack in the US that theoretically might have been avoided.
22. World reaction against "pre-emption" or "anticipatory self-defense" could inhibit the US ability to engage in the future.
23. Adverse reaction to the US could result in the US losing military basing rights in the Gulf and other Muslim countries.
24. Recruiting and financing for terrorist networks could take a dramatic upward turn from successful information operations by our enemies, positioning the US as anti-Muslim.
25. The US will learn, to our surprise, a number of the "unknown unknowns," the gaps in our intelligence

knowledge, for example: Iraqi WMD programs could be several years more advanced than we assessed; Iraqi capabilities of which we were unaware may exist, such as UAVs, jamming, cyber-attacks, etc.; others one might imagine!

26. Fortress Baghdad could prove to be long and unpleasant for all.
27. Iraq could experience ethnic strife among Sunni, Shia, and Kurds.
28. Iraq could use chemical weapons against the Shia and blame the US.
29. Iraq could successfully best us in public relations and persuade the world that the war is against Muslims.

It is well that war is so terrible, otherwise we should grow too fond of it.

Robert E. Lee

God created war so Americans could learn geography.

Mark Twain

It is forbidden to kill; therefore all murderers are punished unless they kill in large numbers and to sound of trumpets.

Voltaire

Only the dead have seen the end of war.

Plato

If this was easy, the French would be doing it.

Steve Jacklin

EPILOGUE

The question of God and the next terminus on this odyssey weighs heavy, no ambiguity or doubts, only wonderment, and curiosity. You cannot experience a magnificent mountain vista, smell the redolent aroma of an orchard in bloom or witness the miracle of childbirth without realizing there is a Divine Hand orchestrating everything seen and unseen.

The ability to see or even understand the Divinity is retarded by the flesh, spiritually confined to the body, opaque in a rational, thoughtful understanding of what is. Only when the being is released from the carnal citadel will all be understood. The apple of knowledge will, at last, be tasted.

With this in mind, I woolgathered the theory of "The Cosmic Cocktail," an attempt to understand what is indistinct and enigmatic, infinite and divine. I've moved to the understanding that the soul is encased in an ice cube. The ice cube is placed in a glass filled with water. The glass is eternity and the water is symbolic of God's omnipresent being. As the ice cube melts, our energy (soul) melts and is absorbed by the water, God's grace. We become one with him for everlasting.

I'm comfortable with this fallible understanding. I am comfortable in the ice cube.

Steve Jacklin

THE COMIC COCKTAIL

*The glass comes filled, with water chilled ... a liquid metaphor
the ice cube floats, an icy moat, inside the Waterford
Stir the ice, the ice will melt ... absorbed by violent storms
until the cube, totally consumed ... becomes eternal norm
Resolutions to ensure, we have a cure ... to purify the ice
as it melts into, the cosmic stew ... with verdict on our vice
The heat is gone, no longer wrong ... is stored inside the cube
judgement passed, and at last ... a peaceful solitude*

*Time corrupts, the water cup ... and the general will
restoring order in the universe ... quiet, motion still
Chaos defaults to a natural state ... master and the slave
the consequence is large, grotesque ... predacious roads, well paved
Age has tempered impertinence ... quiet moments prevail
soul is energy for the universe ... forming the cosmic cocktail
Deist may project another thought ... as we stir the murky mix
to the second ring, what will we bring ... across the River Styx?*

*Once the flesh, renewal fresh ... like the shedding of a snake
focus on, the path to come ... and the one that you forsake
The voyage becomes a bird ... a prey that's looking down
tracking victims, mountain pass ... grassy covered ground
Screams from those, well-disposed ... the smell of burning flesh
melting skin, dissolving sin ... souls that share unrest
Pain and vile, from those exiled ... expel the carnal urge
cannot come in, with all that's been ... trapped inside the cube*

The Journey

Without a respite, or early exit ... as you taste the putrid murk
your eyes convulse, with rapid pulse ... fall into the cirque
No way out, despite the shout ... the echo of pleading cries
just one chance left, to fail the guest ... and vanquish all the lies
With no clocks, or steady vex ... time will just stand still
a friend awash ... in his doubtful cosmic cocktail
Reaching out to touch, fingers clutched ... but he cannot hold
the cube has not yet melted ... purge now what is old

Changes made, to escapades ... and conquest in the past
what is done, cannot become ... the ice that fills the glass
Embrace and touch, the mercy crutch ... with those that went before
resolutions long, fix the wrong ... so you may enter thru the door

Steve Jacklin

Made in the USA
Columbia, SC
21 November 2023